TABLE OF CONTENTS

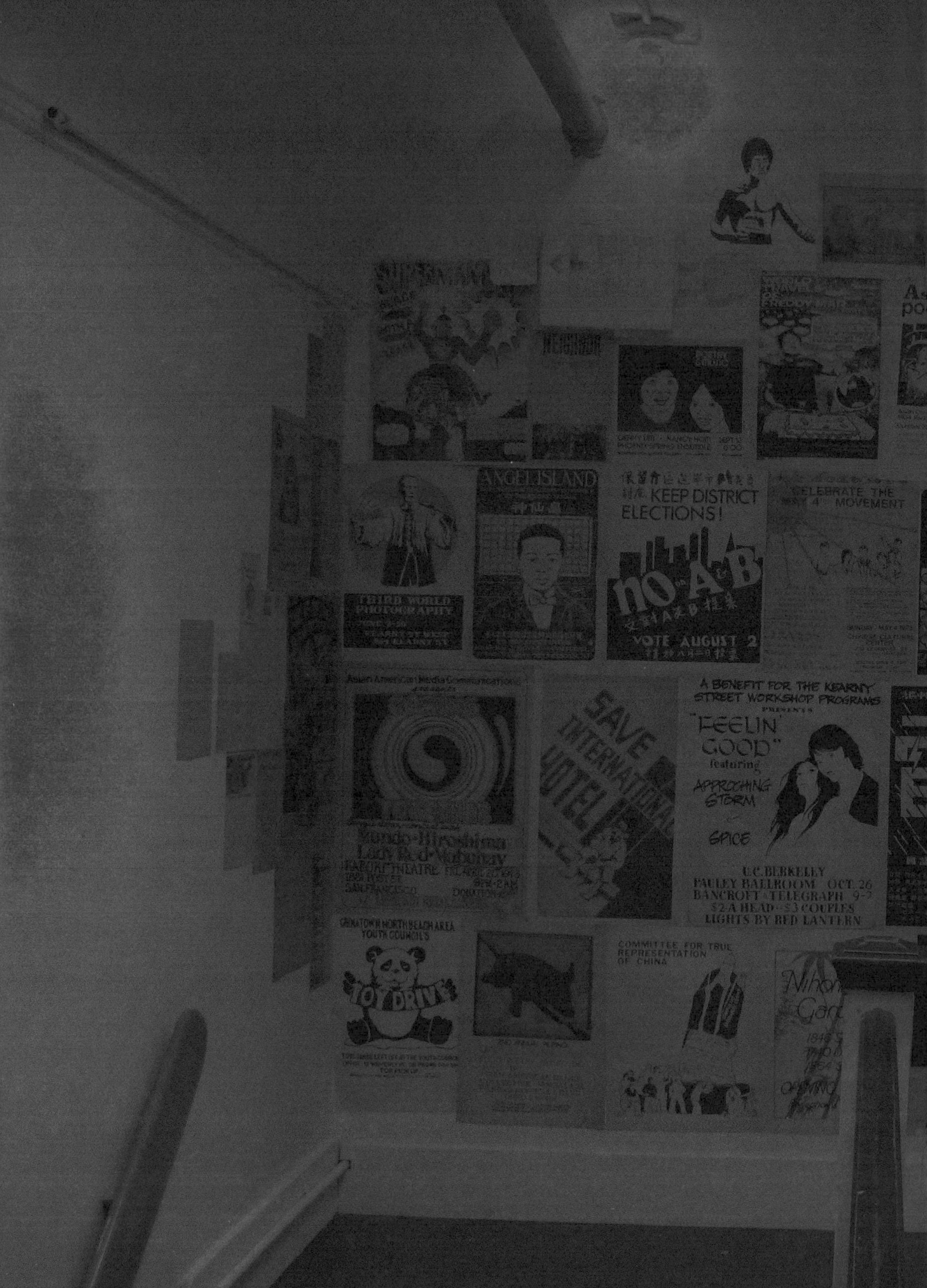

NEIGHBOR
ANGEL ISLAND
THIRD WORLD PHOTOGRAPHY
KEEP DISTRICT ELECTIONS!
no on A & B
VOTE AUGUST 2
CELEBRATE THE MAY 4 MOVEMENT
SAVE INTERNATIONAL HOTEL
A BENEFIT FOR THE KEARNY STREET WORKSHOP PROGRAMS
PRESENTS
"FEELIN' GOOD"
featuring
APPROACHING STORM
SPICE
U.C. BERKELEY
PAULEY BALLROOM   OCT. 26
BANCROFT & TELEGRAPH   9-2
$2 A HEAD · $3 COUPLES
LIGHTS BY RED LANTERN
CHINATOWN NORTH BEACH AREA
YOUTH COUNCILS
TOY DRIVE
COMMITTEE FOR TRUE
REPRESENTATION
OF CHINA

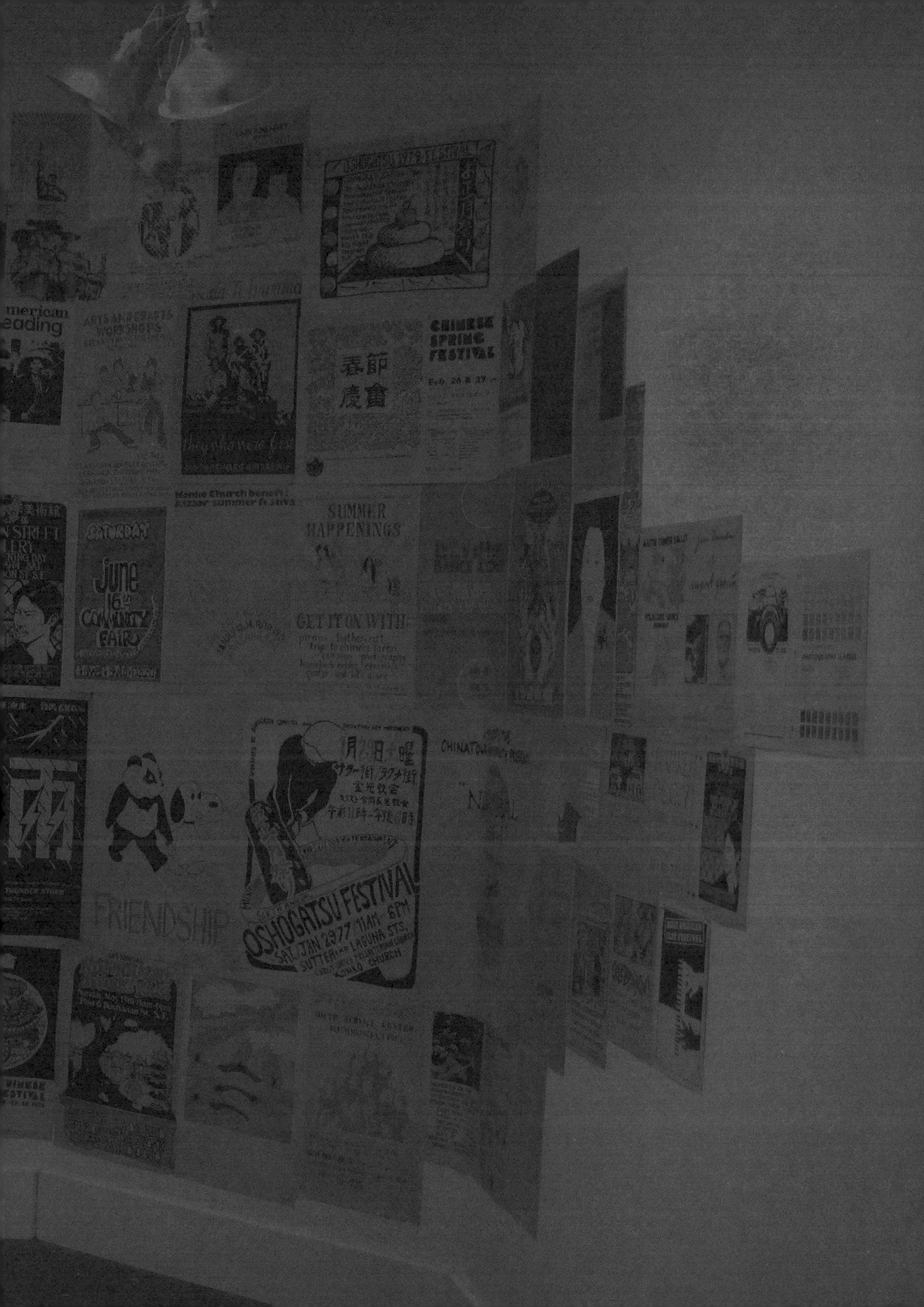

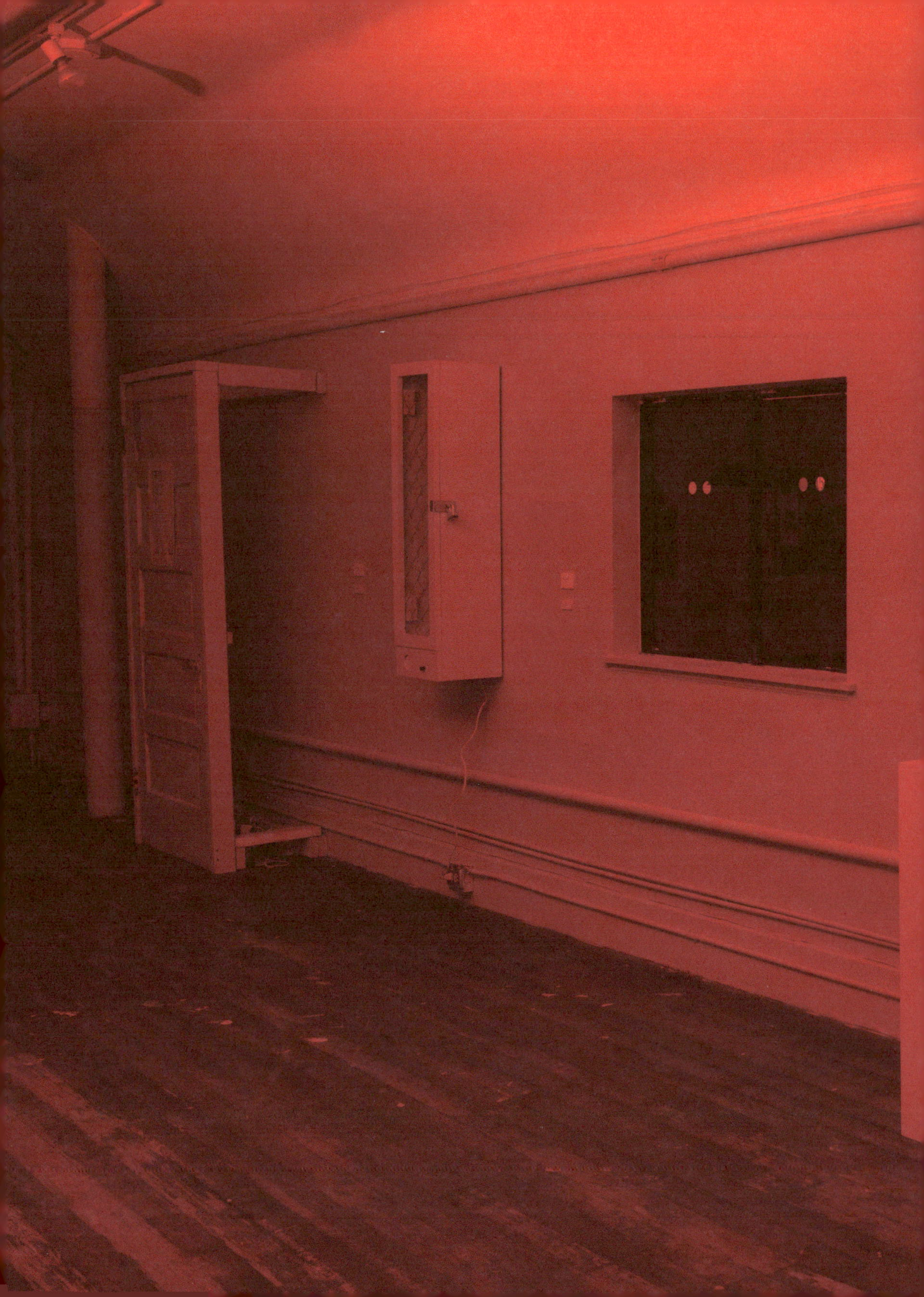

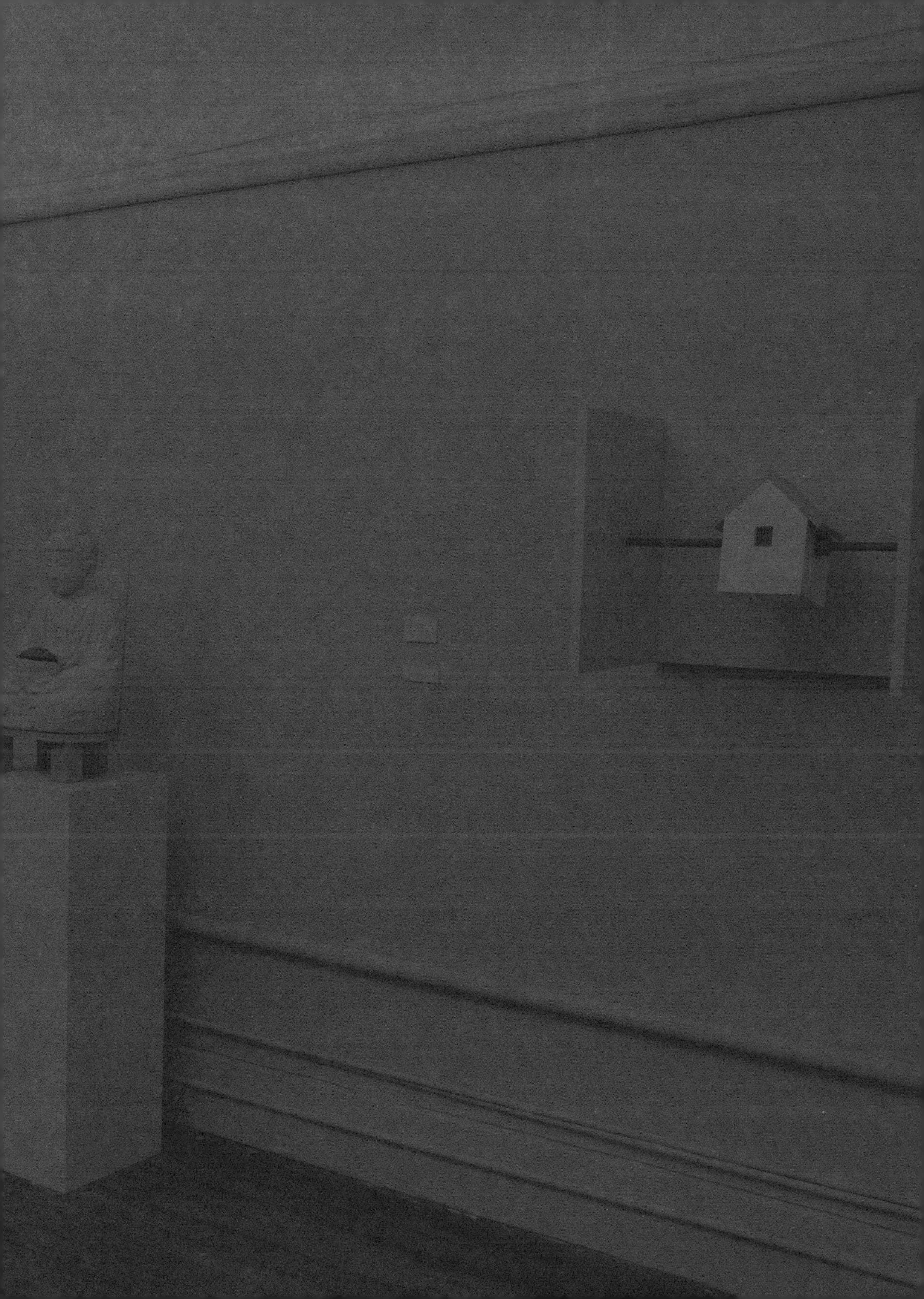

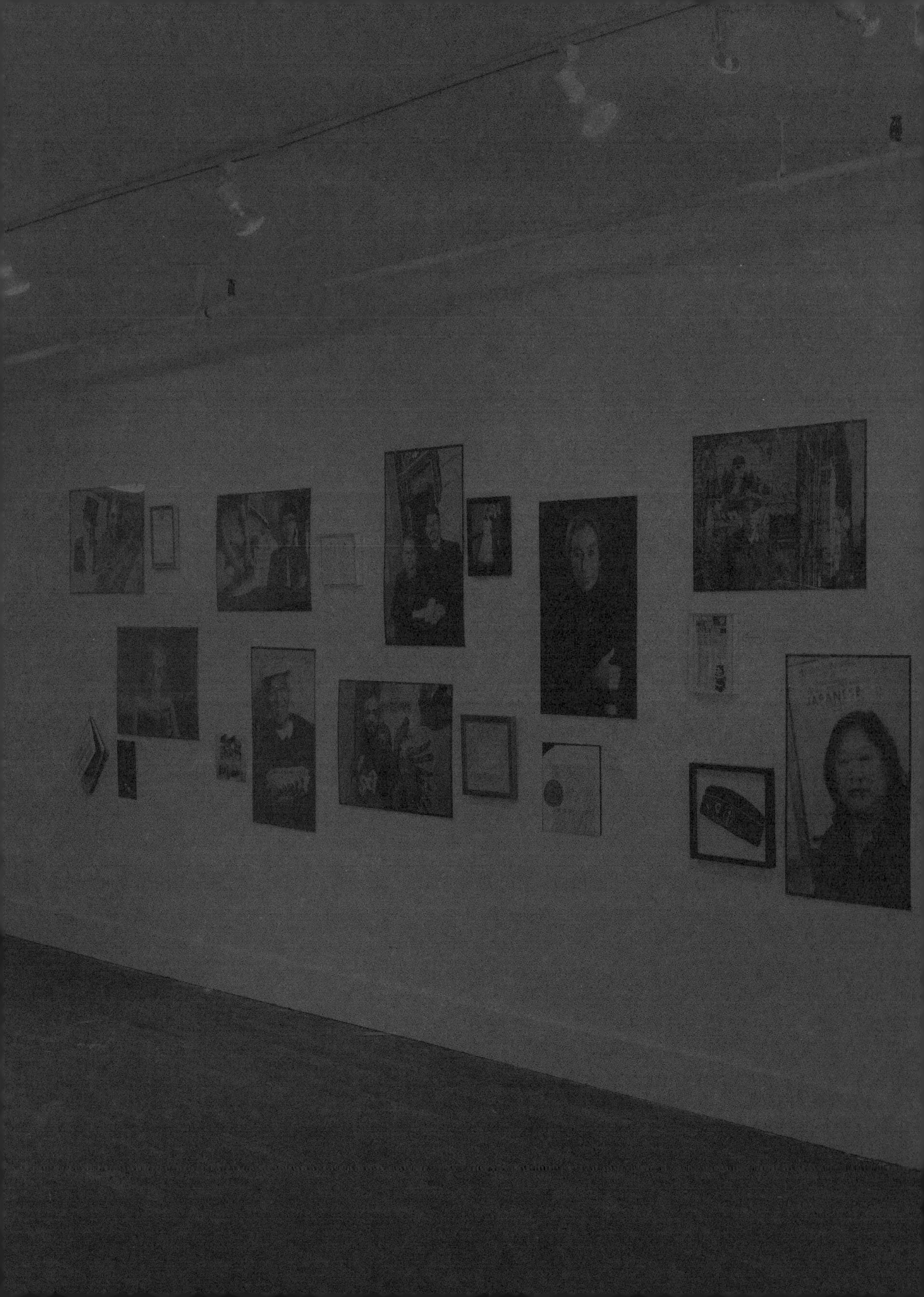

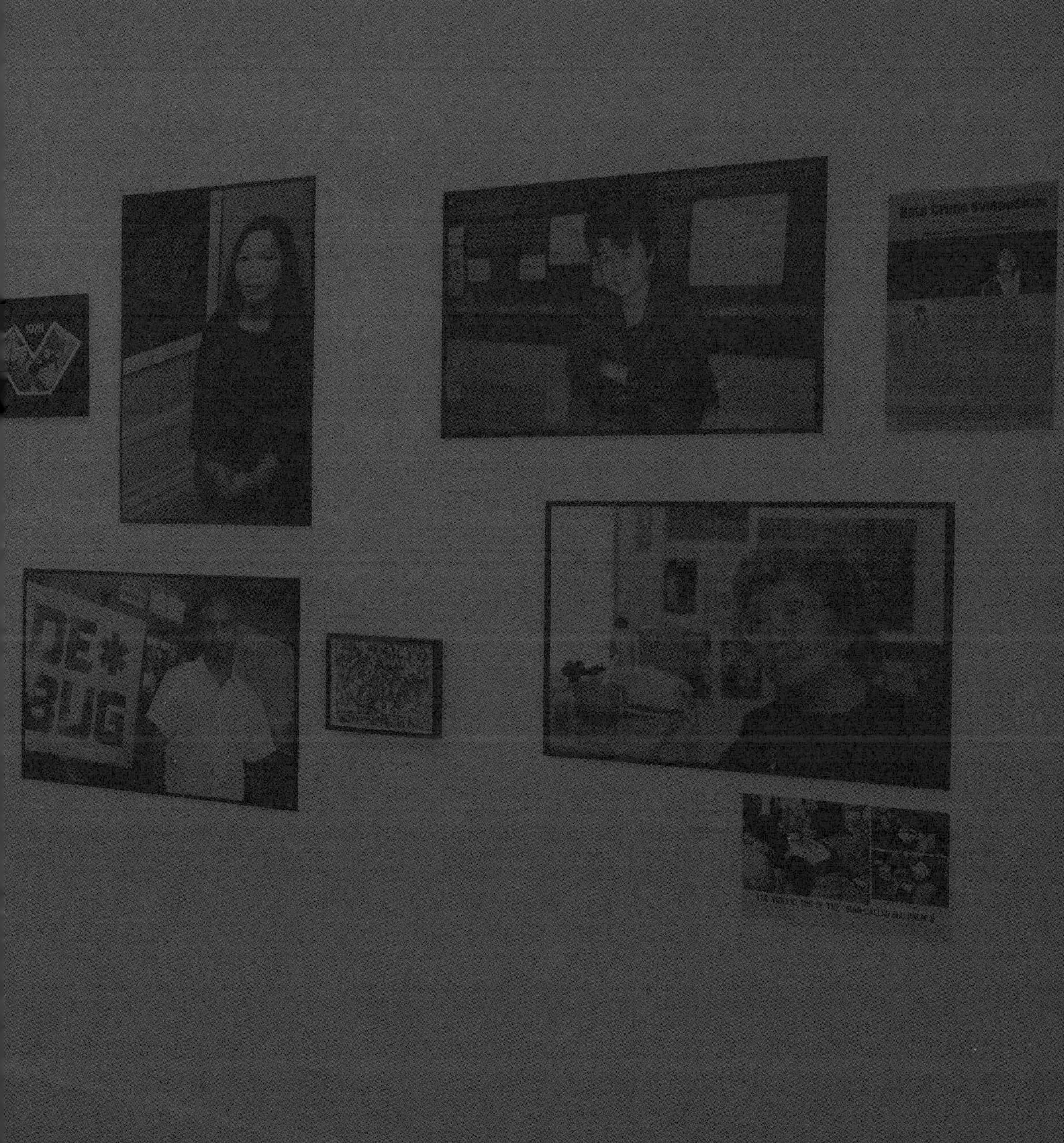

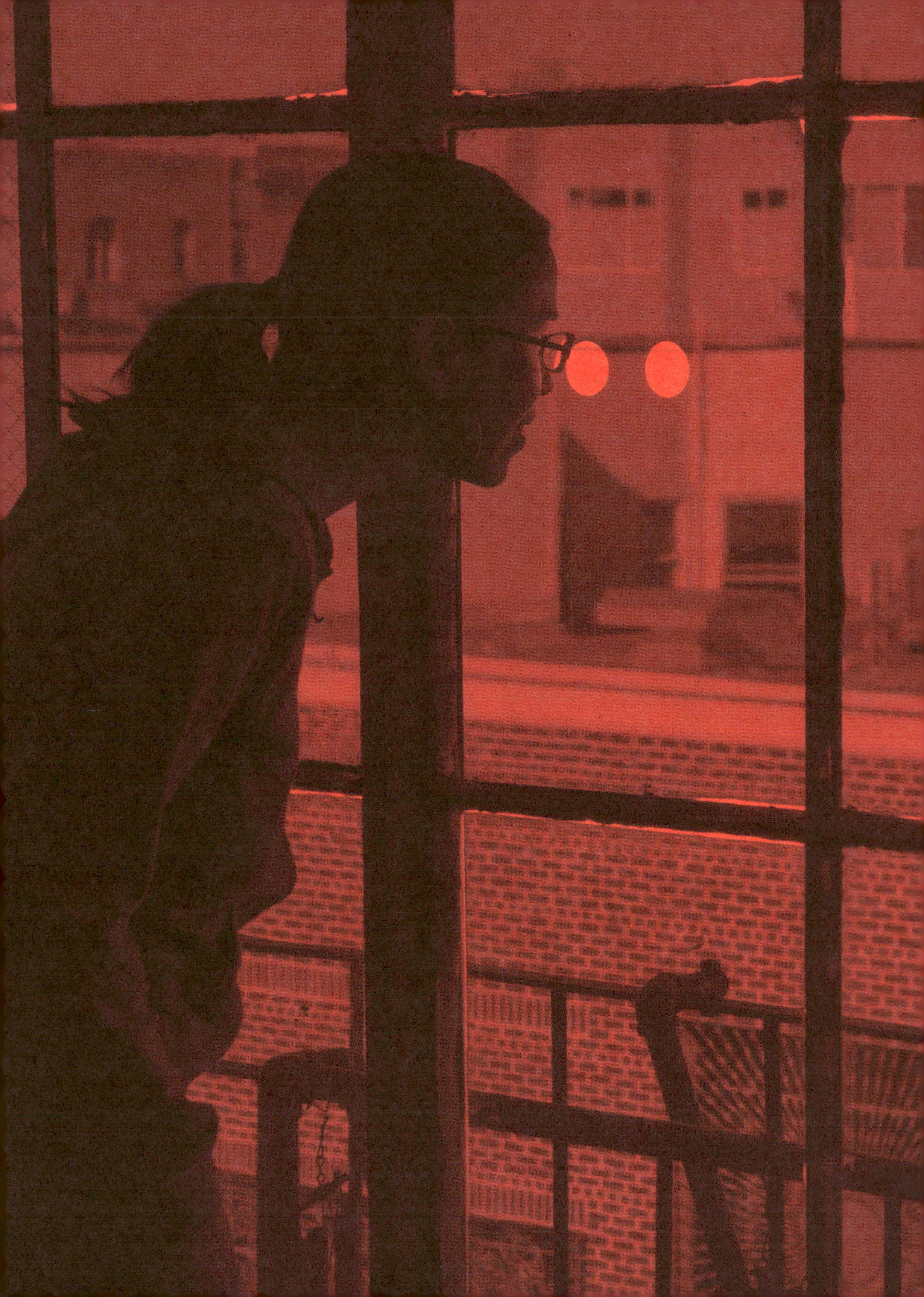

WELCOME TO ACTIVIST IMAGINATION

Kearny Street Workshop officially turned thirty-five in August 2007, and this milestone offers a perfect opportunity to remember, celebrate, and create.

KSW was founded on Kearny Street in 1972, and since then we have made ourselves a home on a number of other, non-Kearny Street, addresses. We've found ourselves in Chinatown, North Beach, South Park, SOMA, and now, most recently, the Mission District of San Francisco. Through all the different streets and neighborhoods, however, the legacy of KSW's earliest years at its first home, the I-Hotel, endures, continuing to inform and shape our identity.

But KSW could never exist in a state of suspended animation. Enriched and surely emboldened by its past, KSW is constantly transforming and reinventing itself, celebrating and investigating migration and the fluid nature of boundaries rather than attempting to enforce rigid and arbitrary lines of identity. We find, in fact, that relocating across miles and years can have the effect of strengthening a spirit of connectedness; there is something about movement, forced or voluntary, that affirms a sense of home and community.

So what does any of this have to do with the *Activist Imagination* project, and with this book?

On the occasion of our 35th anniversary — and in keeping with the wisdom of knowing where we've been so we can know where we're going — we wanted to honor and celebrate the history of the organization while challenging ourselves to examine the world around us and imagine what lies ahead.

So we wanted to look at where we've been, investigate where we are today, and look at where we're going. And we wanted to do it all through the lens of KSW's spirit of activism, a spirit in which KSW is firmly rooted in spite of all the changes and reinventions. For many in KSW's past and present, activism has not been a lifestyle choice, but an imperative for living in this world, and, as panelist Oscar Peñaranda said in a November 2007 conversation, "activism and being an artist is kind of the same; it comes from the same source at least."

Of course, there are other perspectives on activism and art, and we as a community are host to an unlimited number of points of view and experiences. We wanted to create a space and a program that honored all these differences and allowed for a complex and nuanced dialogue that looks backwards, forwards, and all around.

Activist Imagination seeks to explore the past, present and future of activism, the arts, and community, incorporating three major components:

KSW's History: KSW's thirty-five years of archives, including silk-screened posters, photographs, audio and videotapes, and publications. These archives were made available to the lead visual artists over the course of the project.

Discussion Series: A series of panel discussions about the past, present, and future of activism, the arts, and community, featuring prominent artists and activists based in the San Francisco Bay Area. The discussion series also features an on-line conversation, in the shape of the *Activist Imagination* blog, maintained by the artists and KSW. Community members were invited to attend and participate in the free discussion series and view and post comments on the blog.

Visual Exhibiton: A gallery show featuring new work created as a response to the subject matter, the archives, and the discussion series.

For the third component, we invited three artists from different walks of life, working in different media, and with markedly different takes on activism and being an artist, to use their art to respond to the subject of activism, the arts, and community, and KSW's thirty-five years of history.

The work they created, a sample of the discussions that took place, and a glimpse into the archives via one artist's contribution, are represented here in these pages. While not a complete record, we hope that this book captures the spirit of the *Activist Imagination* project, and provides plenty of fodder for further thought and debate.

During one of the *Activist Imagination* discussions in March 2008, one of the panelists, choreographer Erika Chong Shuch, said something of particular resonance:

> *I feel the world is just falling apart and I don't have an enormous amount of faith and hope. I want to see people act up. I want to see people be unreasonable and make crazy demands. I want to see people make a lot of noise, and I want to see a future where young people feel inspired and impassioned to value their own stories and to value their own creativity. Because I think the problems we're facing globally are problems we're going to have to fix through creative means. We're going to have to invoke that creative spirit in order to imagine a new world.*

Erika articulates what I feel is at the core of the *Activist Imagination* project — the power of art to both illuminate the world around us and to imagine a better world. Many of us are looking around wondering what the hell is going on, and how much worse things are going to get before they start getting better — or if they ever will at all. Creative expression gives our spirits and our imaginations the flexibility and resilience necessary to consider alternate realities. Given our world and the present and near-future state of things, what choice do we really have but to imagine, and to act?

To each of the artists and participants, thank you for sharing your time, talent, and imagination, and for approaching this project and this world with an open mind and a willingness to consider new possibilities.

And thanks to you, the reader, for picking up and experiencing this book.

MIND THE GAP
KEVIN B. CHEN

Mind The Gap

Something artist Christine Wong Yap had said in regards to the ideas informing her role in *Activist Imagination* stuck with me: *I wanted to challenge the idea that somehow as an artist I'm special enough to imagine the future of activism, but in reality you or any other viewer has the same ability to affect the future of activism as anybody else.* Her invitation offers an interesting glimpse into KSW's year-long project. *Activist Imagination* doesn't have a mono-lithic tone or singular perspective on what it means to stand at the intersection of activism, arts, and community. Rather, the exhibition embraces a number of art practices that are as diverse as the methods of activism themselves. Each of the three participating artists — Bob Hsiang, Donna Keiko Ozawa, and Christine Wong Yap — employs contrasting artistic strategies to communicate their particular take on the challenge posed to them months ago by KSW in anticipation of its 35th anniversary.

This isn't an easy exhibition to digest. The combination of three very distinct voices and ap-proaches to exploring the scope and overlap of activism, arts, and community may trigger complicated responses in viewers, presenting several ripe opportunities to dig deeper and ask why as viewers we either get or don't get certain works.

Some comment on how "common folk" and contemporary art usually don't mix, and how conventional forms of activist art just don't generate anything new or original anymore. Does conceptual art have the capacity to inspire the masses? Can traditional activist art excite contemporary art audiences? Although different strategies are employed in the production of both conceptual art and traditional activist art, common ground can be found amongst the two. Each tries to engage audiences in ideas broader than the formal aspects of the artwork itself — be it issues of resolving economic disparity or questioning how one sees the world. Although there are significant differences in how form and function operate within these two strategies, each essentially asks the viewer to remain open and receptive to the ideas being put forth. Art, regardless of its conceptual or activist bent, frequently challenges viewers to question and re-evaluate their assumptions, predispositions, and beliefs. Art isn't intrinsically educational, but the possibility for new perspectives and broadened horizons exists with the viewing of each piece of art. You may not understand what an artist is trying to say with his or her work. You may not even like it aesthetically. But if you attempt to approach a work of art with an engaged curiosity that is respectful and not immediately contemptuous, you may at least come away from the viewing experience with an awareness that your ultimate dislike or incomprehension of a piece of art doesn't have to be solely based on subjective knee-jerk reaction.

In *Activist Imagination*, the overall combination of work by Hsiang, Ozawa, and Wong Yap asks us to check our potentially impulsive responses at the door and to be on good behavior, as Wong Yap reminds us in her piece *The Best Person I Can Be*. In *Activist Imagination*, we are presented with a mixture of conceptual art and activist art, instigated by both the subject matter and influence of KSW's legacy, yet approaching both subject and legacy with extremely varied perspectives. This synthesized location of conceptual art and activist art is precisely where *Activist Imagination* finds its strengths. To attempt to get at the past, present and future of activism, arts, and community, as the exhibition's broad title posits, there needs to be a number of approaches and languages to illustrate the broad interconnectedness of these issues. What worked before might not necessarily work now, and what works now might not necessarily work in the future.

Picturing Activism

Bob Hsiang's collective photographic portrait of Bay Area APA activists and activist artists provides an important, grounding framework for the exhibition. As someone who for over thirty years helped to shape and document the seminal movement to locate and articulate an Asian American social and cultural identity, Hsiang provides a living link to the rich history of the confluence of APA arts, activism, and community, not only through his person but also through the lens of his camera. His portraits of thirteen individuals (including painters, performers, activists, poets, attorneys, journalists, and designers) look and feel heroic; indeed, many are larger than life-size. The dignity and self-assurance with which they individually hold themselves form a composite that collectively lands their gaze into the camera and onto the viewer in the gallery — not in a confrontational way, but rather one that asks the viewer to engage a bit deeper, to stretch to find out more about their presence in the room. Hsiang's work underscores an often assumed, yet taken for granted, component to activism — that the desire for social and political change begins with the selfless dedication of individual people to make a difference. Movements, after all, start with people.

Each person is located within the frame in a larger physical context that rounds out the portrait — in the studio, in front of city hall, in front of historical material. The photographic style is very straightforward, as there isn't much insertion of Hsiang's hand into the picture. Yet, each person exudes a level of comfort with the camera, emphasizing Hsiang's standing and reputation in the community. He has known many of these artists and activists for decades stemming back to the early days of KSW; others he has met only in recent years through programs such as KSW's *APAture* festival. The work truly represents a historical lineage, in form, content, and intent. The work is ostensibly not about Hsiang the photographer, but rather about the community of individuals who have committed themselves to a life of soliciting change.

In both Donna Keiko Ozawa and Christine Wong Yap's work, viewer interaction is required for the completion of the works. In two of Ozawa's works (*Robbie was there I* and *Robbie was there II*), she references Richard Hongisto, a figure notorious both in the organizational history of KSW and in her own personal history through the direct use of prefabricated objects. She additionally uses humor to make her other two works more accessible to the audience. *Weather Buddha* looks at the unintended consequences of activism, the propensity for fatigue and burnout, and comments upon a growing number of activists turning towards Buddhism as a means of revitalization and sustenance. The large button that activates the sound of a real-time weather report station is meant to parallel the continually changing tide of political and cultural currents to the continuously shifting conditions of the weather. The fourth piece that Ozawa features in *Activist Imagination*, *Sheep House*, is also one that invites physical interaction. Ozawa has developed a large body of work that employs the hand crank, a crude analog mechanism for effecting movement. Framed against a backdrop of an archetypal blue sky sits a bland yellow model house. Turning the crank rotates the house on its axis, and simultaneously amplifies sheep bleating from a noisemaker toy located inside the sculpture. She questions the American ideal of success and happiness as manifested in the goal of owning or living in a standard home, and wonders if one's political ideals and beliefs get disjointed in the process of pursuing this.

Christine Wong Yap's work is the most conceptually based in the exhibition. She contributes three art pieces (*The Best Person I Can Be,* untitled site-specific window installation, *Seeing Red*) and one curatorial project — reproductions of early KSW posters and flyers lining the hallway leading up to the gallery. Her main approach was to design the work to be inherently about the viewer. In a way, she removes her own hand in order to place the viewer as the central, necessary agent in the work. Wong Yap's own points of view and ideologies aren't clearly located within her work; rather she positions the responsibility of determining meaning and intent directly back upon the viewer. Her work is a visual platform upon which the viewer completes the circuit of the idea. *The Best Person I Can Be* is the first piece that viewers encounter upon entering the main gallery, providing a framework for literal and metaphoric reflection for everyone who enters. The piece consists of a constructed room, the interior of which allows viewers to see a reflection of themselves superimposed on those standing on the other side of the mirror, creating the possibility to see oneself reflected in other people — an essential tenet in activist movements. As well, the other two pieces are based in visual perception. Wong Yap's belief that anyone can shape the future of activism, artist or not, is underscored by her use of tinted film. One's view of the world can be a driving force towards participation in activist movements, and she posits how a viewer sees the outside world through the contrast of dark tinted window film and pairs of rose-colored peepholes inserted into select darkened window panes. Do you see the world as dark and pessimistic, full of cynicism and distrust, or is there clarity and optimism that drives your engagement with the world? What emotional and psychological elements spur individuals to action? Wong Yap's articulations of her ideas are very economical — austere materials and simple design allow far-reaching questions to be posed without extraneous or distracting ornament.

Laying The Foundation

Now, more than four decades after a number of visionary artists and activists carved out an articulation of what would become known as Asian American theatre, literature, visual art, music, dance, and film, we can look back and see how substantial and diverse this body of work has grown. An integral part of this history on both a regional and national scale, KSW has provided countless opportunities for then emerging artists to cultivate and share their work with each other and the larger community. Building community through art has always been a backbone of KSW's mission, and one of the most tangible, enduring legacies borne out of the early years of KSW that continues today. In 1999, KSW presented the first *APAture,* a multi-disciplinary festival showcasing the work of emerging Asian Pacific American (APA) artists that now, in its tenth year, has proven to be instrumental in rendering KSW relevant to a younger generation of artists, activists and community members. Even though the socio-political landscape is substantially different now than over three decades ago, the work featured in the first nine years of *APAture* has been considerably of the contemporary and experimental bent. Is it that a younger generation of artists within the APA community is not as interested in working within activism, or is it because of the many strides and battles fought over the decades by an earlier generation that has made this type of experimentation possible?

The APA experience is as diverse as human experience itself, and its cultural manifestations are as wide-ranging as culture itself. The expansive cultural lineage that spans from filmmakers Wayne Wang to Michael Kang, authors Maxine Hong Kingston to Jeff Chang, playwrights Frank Chin to Diana Son, musicians Glenn Horiuchi to Jin, visual artists Martin Wong to

Anna Sew Hoy — a group of artists as varied in their conceptual and activist practices as the particular social, political, and cultural contexts in which each created their work — underscores how broad a definition of APA culture can and ought to be. Yet, we should continue to acknowledge those who have paved the path towards self-realization and self-expression. Without their struggle to carve out an identity distinct from mainstream America, many younger APA artists simply wouldn't have the license to create as freely and as experimentally as they do now, and to approach strategies of conceptual or activist art on their own terms.

Kevin B. Chen is an artist and curator who has lived in the Bay Area since 1994 and for close to a decade has been one of the Program Directors at Intersection for the Arts, one of the country's oldest alternative non-profit art spaces. His work has been exhibited at KSW over the years, including *APAture* (2000), *Limited Edition: Recent Work By Emerging Asian Pacific American Artists* (2001), and *Home* (2006).

15
ACTIVIST IMAGINATION
THE PROJECT

Activist Imagination is an exhibition and series of discussions investigating, exploring, and imagining the past, present, and future of activism. In keeping with its own history of engaging community issues through art, KSW defines activism to be "any form of civic engagement intended to effect social change." The project's intent was to investigate various forms of activism over the last thirty-five years, and to envision creative new forms and expressions of activism that might hold meaning and relevance in the future.

Kearny Street Workshop collaborated with artists Donna Keiko Ozawa, Bob Hsiang, and Christine Wong Yap, to create a new multimedia exhibition responding to the themes of activism, the arts, and community. The exhibition — the culmination of a year-long exploration of this broadly-conceived notion of activism by Ozawa, Hsiang, and Wong Yap — took place February 29 - May 24, 2008, at KSW's space180 in the Mission District of San Francisco. The artists explored activism's past, through KSW's 35 years of archived materials commemorating the Asian American movement, and its present, through a quarterly open discussion series involving KSW's network of artists and activists, and through an *Activist Imagination* blog. The discussion series took place November 27, 2007 – April 24, 2008.

The *Activist Imagination* project was made possible in part by a grant from the Creative Work Fund through support from the Walter and Elise Haas Fund, The William and Flora Hewlett Foundation, and the James Irvine Foundation. *Activist Imagination* is also supported in part by a grant from the San Francisco Foundation and by KSW's members and individual donors.

The project: *http://www.kearnystreet.org/activistimagination*
The blog: *http://kearnystreet.wordpress.com/category/activist-imagination/*

BOB HSIANG

DONNA KEIKO OZAWA

CHRISTINE WONG YAP

Bob Hsiang

My own work has been a reflection of the development of Asian American activist art/politics. As Asian American artists and activists, we view/ed all art as political; art serves to either de facto affirm the status quo or revolt against it. This is what I've always found fascinating from a photographer's point of view.

My interest in community activism dates to the late 1960s and early 1970s, when many Asian Americans underwent a major transformation in political and social consciousness as they graduated high schools or college. Having experienced the Cold War, the Kennedy and MLK assassinations, the carnage of the Vietnam War, and the Civil Rights Movement, this generation rebelled against the silence and complicity of an earlier decade. This change ran parallel to the manifestation of the Black Panthers, the anti-Vietnam War movement and the feminist/gay/lesbian revolution that was sweeping the nation. Using the still camera as a tool for change and encouraging people to view the world in an alternative way, I photographed many events held by Asian American students, workers and professionals that reflected the dissatisfaction with the status quo.

I have worked with Kearny Street Workshop for over thirty years. It was at the International Hotel where I met many friends and artists involved in the struggle for tenants' rights and Asian American issues. I was honored to be invited to participate in the *Activist Imagination* project, and I chose to do a photographic exploration of the subject. Since I had photographed many people from all walks of life who have dedicated their lives to activism, this project seemed like a natural fit. After much planning, I selected thirteen subjects I have admired in their search for society's betterment, from those active during the late 1960s to those engaged today. Activism can take many forms: an artist concerned over perceived injustices or contradictions; a community organizer's desire to see change; or an attorney working in the legal system and using Constitutional law to fight discrimination. Hence my collection of images encompasses a wide range of activists.

There are many people who could not be included in this sampling of activists. Hopefully, this series is only a beginning in celebrating those in the Asian American community who have fought with their counterparts in all communities for equality and social justice.

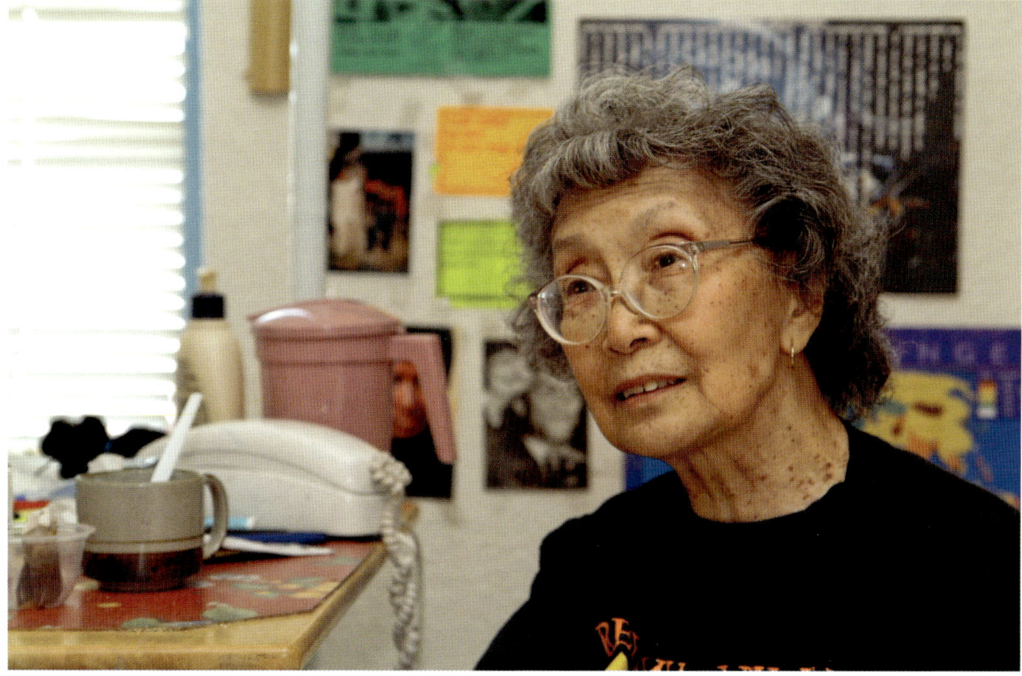

ABOVE AND PAGES 19-25:
PORTRAITS OF 13 ACTIVISTS
2008
digital c-prints
20 x 30 in., and various sizes

These photographs of 13 activists represent a sampling of Asian Americans who have consciously dedicated themselves to the cause of social justice and the protestations against racism, war, environmental destruction and other harmful elements upon our planet. This selection of subjects illustrates a variety of ways in which one can be an activist. Each of them also submitted an artifact that inspired or symbolized his or her activism.

– *Bob Hsiang*

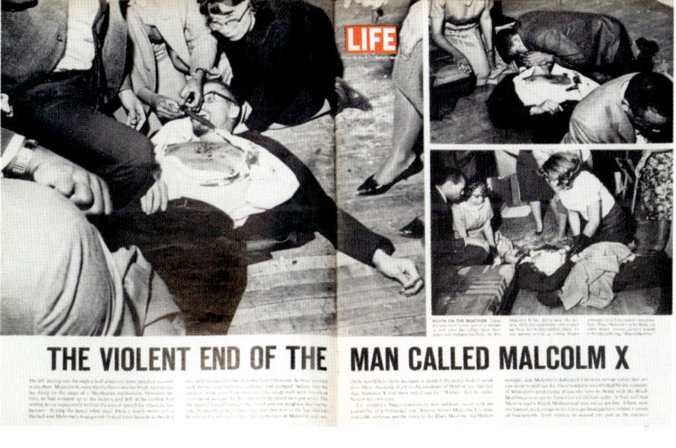

Yuri Kochiyama
Activist, Speaker
Artifact: Copy of *Life* Magazine article on the assassination of Malcolm X, 1964
Yuri's friendship with Malcolm X shaped her views on race relations and the civil rights struggles from the 1960s to the present.

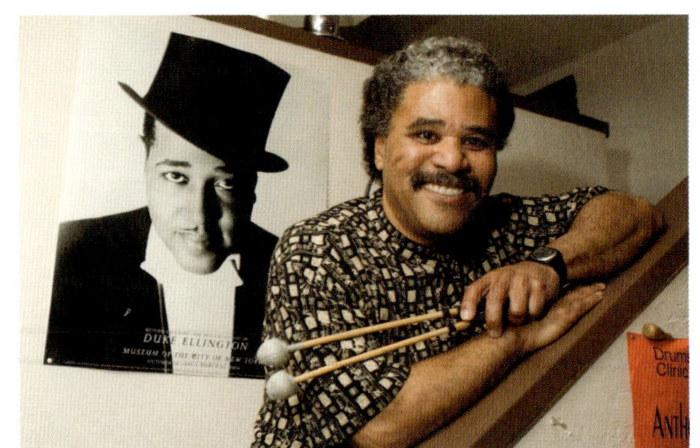

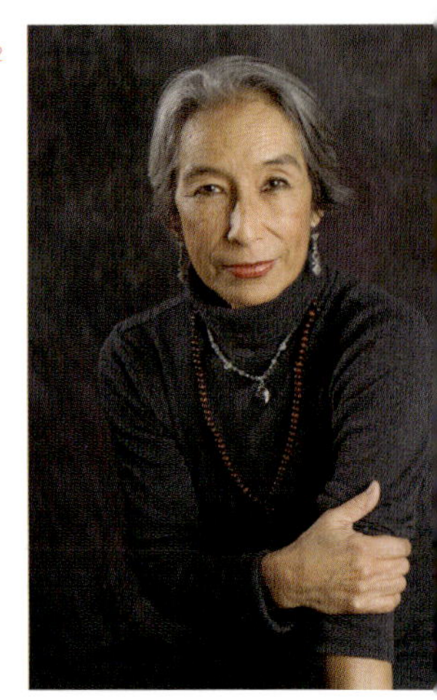

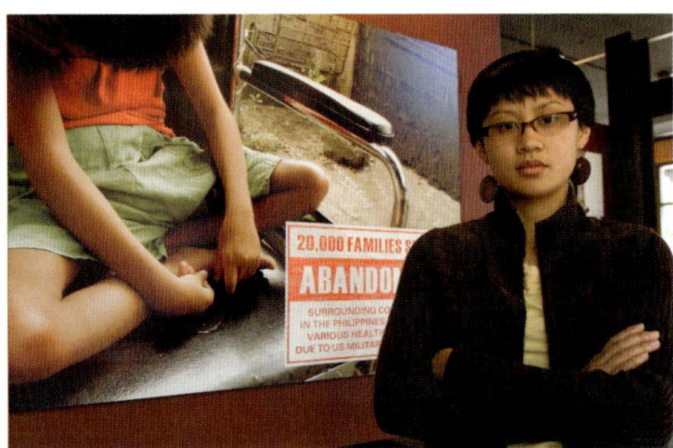

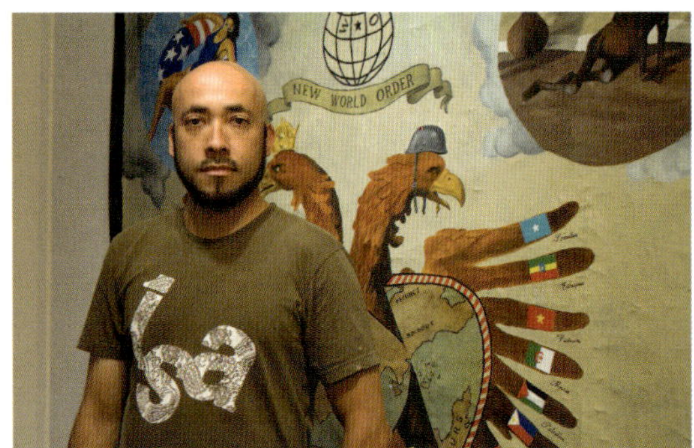

1. Anthony Brown
Composer, Musician
*Artifact: S.F. Board of Supervisors proclamation, 2005
The Asian American Jazz Orchestra was a pioneer
jazz ensemble that addressed issues of multiculturalism.

2. Nobuko Miyamoto
Dancer, Choreographer, Songwriter, Singer
*Artifact: Grain of Sand album cover, 1973
This groundbreaking collection of Asian American folk
music by Nobuko, Chris Iijima and Charlie Chin inspired
generations of Asian American activists.

3. Emalyn Lopez
Photographer
*Artifact: *On Beauty and Being Just* by Elaine Scarry, 1999
"This book is a foundation and driving force in my continued
efforts to search for social and environmental justice."

4. Rick Godinez
Painter, Educator
*Artifact: Hebrew calligraphy and English translation, 1998
This inspirational quote was given to Rick by his dear friend
Jason Francisco.

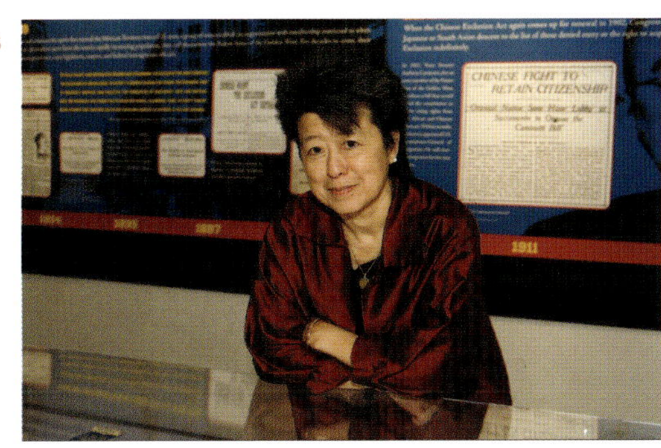

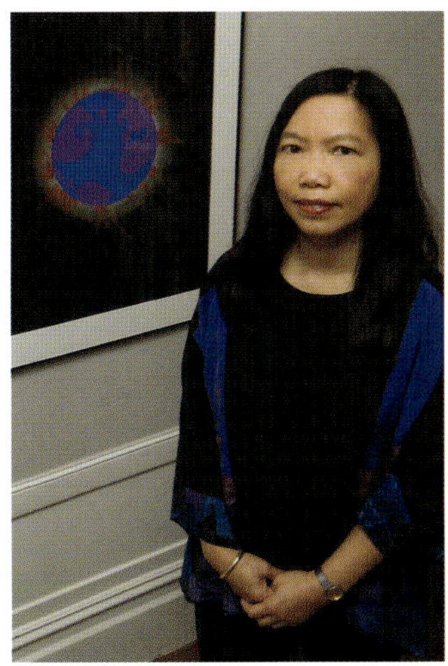

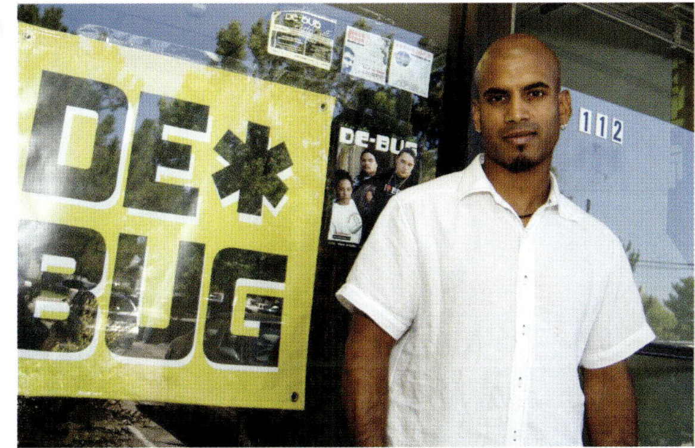

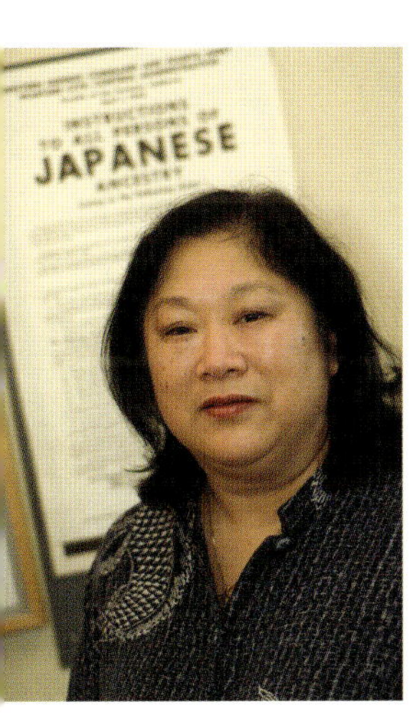

5. Nancy Hom
   Artist, Writer, Curator
   *<u>Artifact</u>: International Hotel calendar, 1978
   The I-Hotel tenants' struggle for low-income housing
   has had a major influence on Nancy since the 1970s.

6. Helen Zia
   Author, Journalist, Activist
   *<u>Artifact</u>: Vincent Chin poster, 1983
   Vincent Chin was a victim of the hatred toward Asians in
   the U.S. during the automakers' financial downturn in
   the late 1970s.

7. Karen Narasaki
   Civil Rights Attorney
   *<u>Artifact</u>: Father's Nisei Vets club hat, 1944
   Karen's father was a WWII veteran whose 442nd brigade
   helped to liberate France from Nazi Germany.

8. Raj Jayadev
   Community Organizer, Publisher
   *<u>Artifact</u>: *De-Bug* magazine: San Jose Rising issue, 2006
   De-Bug offers the Silicon Valley community alternative news
   concerning police harassment, education, and social justice.

Artifacts for portraits 1 - 8 not pictured here

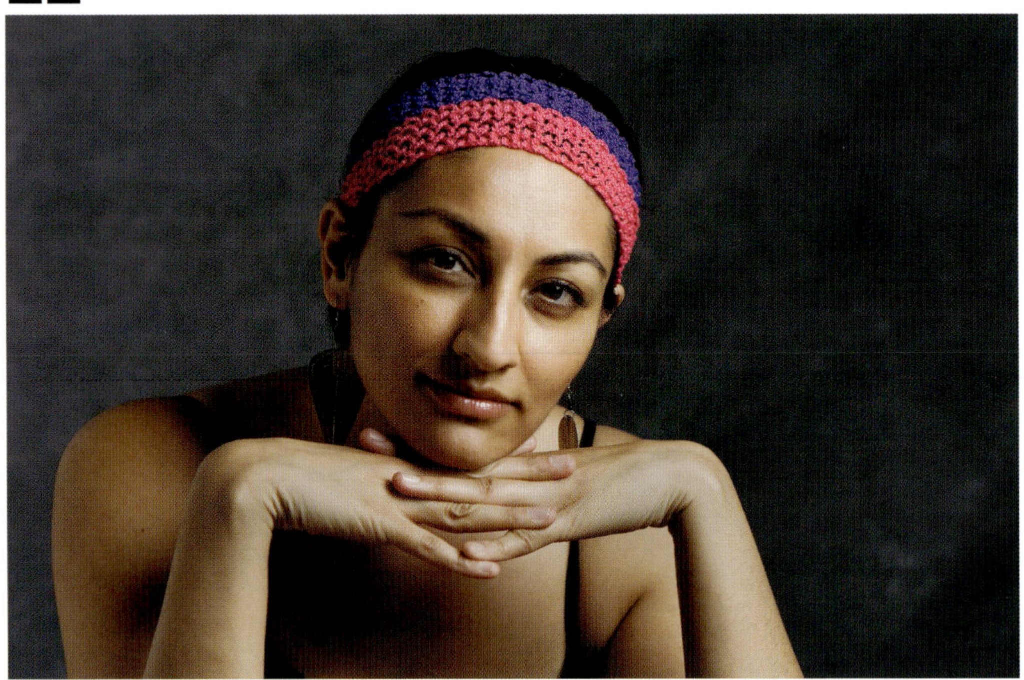

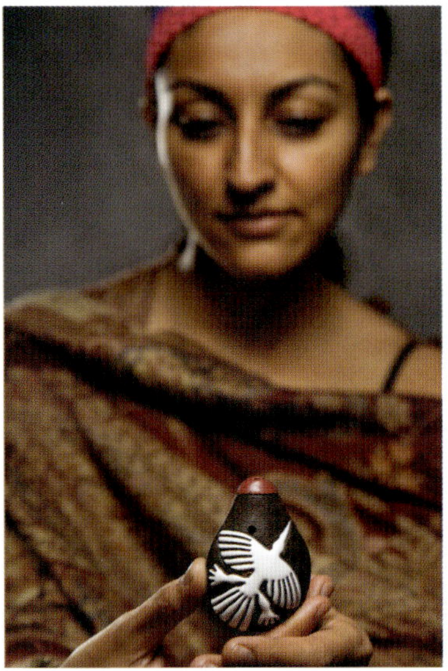

Shailja Patel
Poet, Writer
<u>Artifact</u>: Bird of Joy and Rage, sculptural object
"I carry it with me wherever I tour, to remind me of the power of art to transcend barriers of language, culture, race, and history."

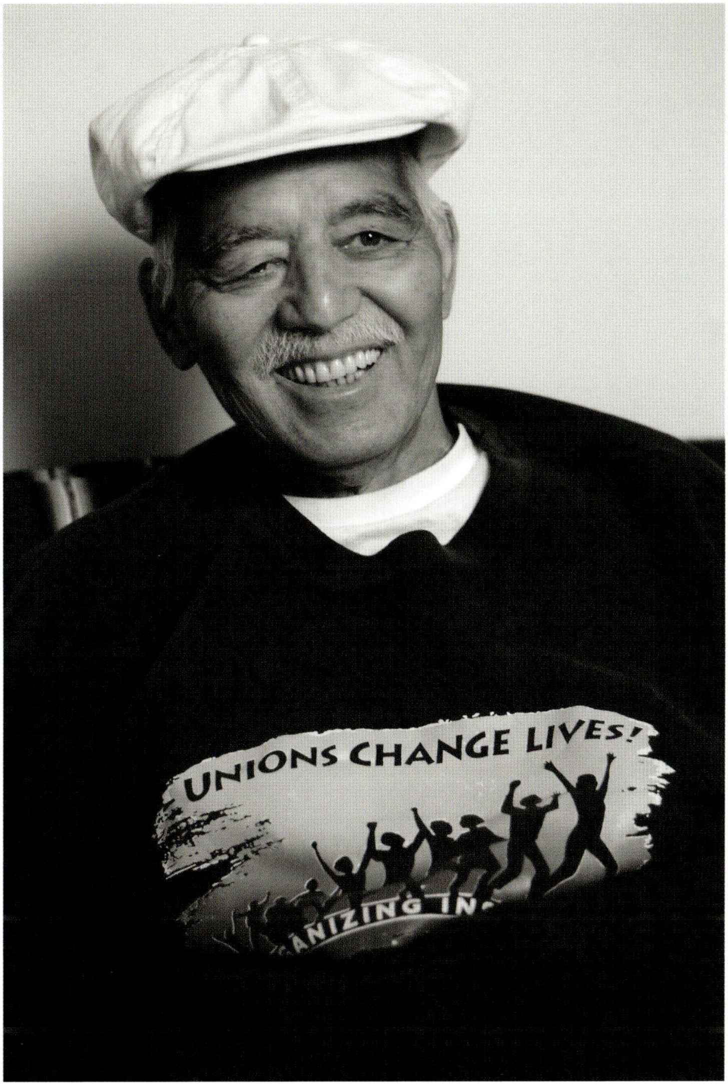

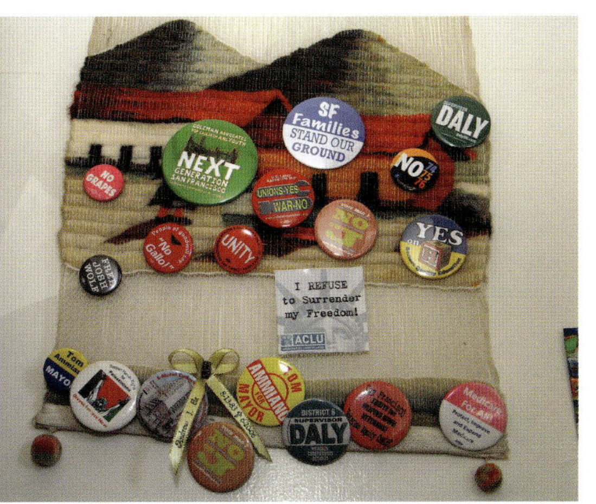

Bill Sorro
Union and Tenants' Rights Activist
<u>Artifact</u>: Buttons on Bill's refrigerator
Bill championed many labor, social justice, and housing
rights causes for decades until he passed away in 2007.

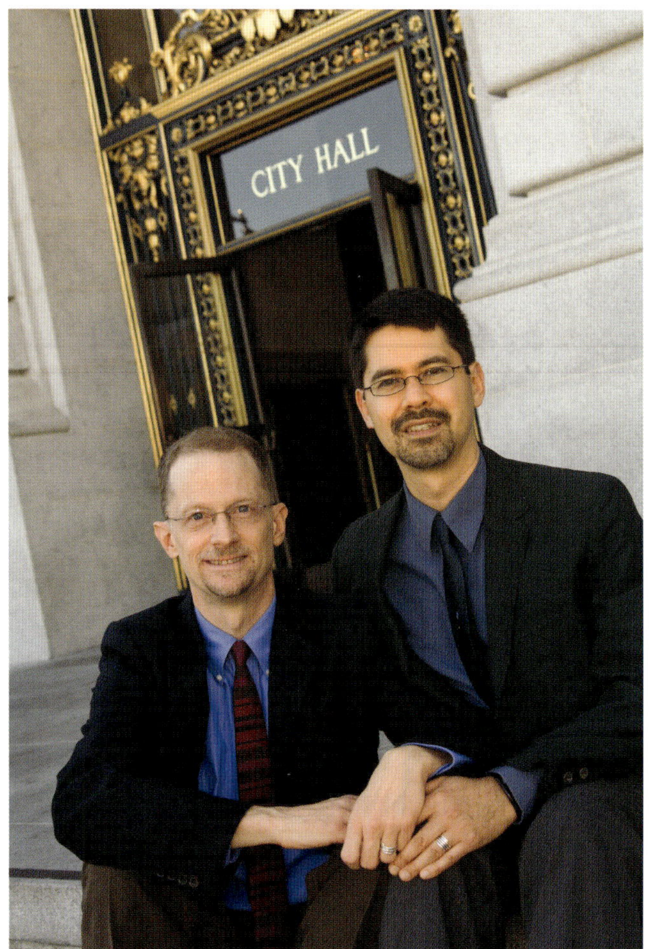

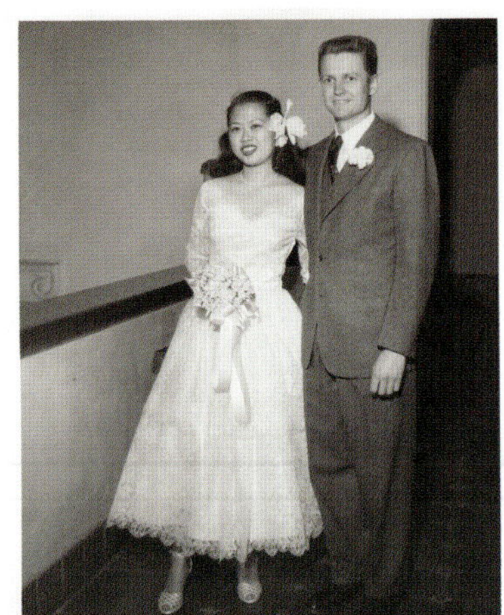

Stuart Gaffney (on the right, with marriage partner John Lewis)
Gay Rights Advocate
<u>Artifact</u>: Parents' wedding photo, 1958
During the 1950s and '60s, anti-miscegenation laws prohibited mixed
couples to wed until the state laws were finally repealed in 1967.

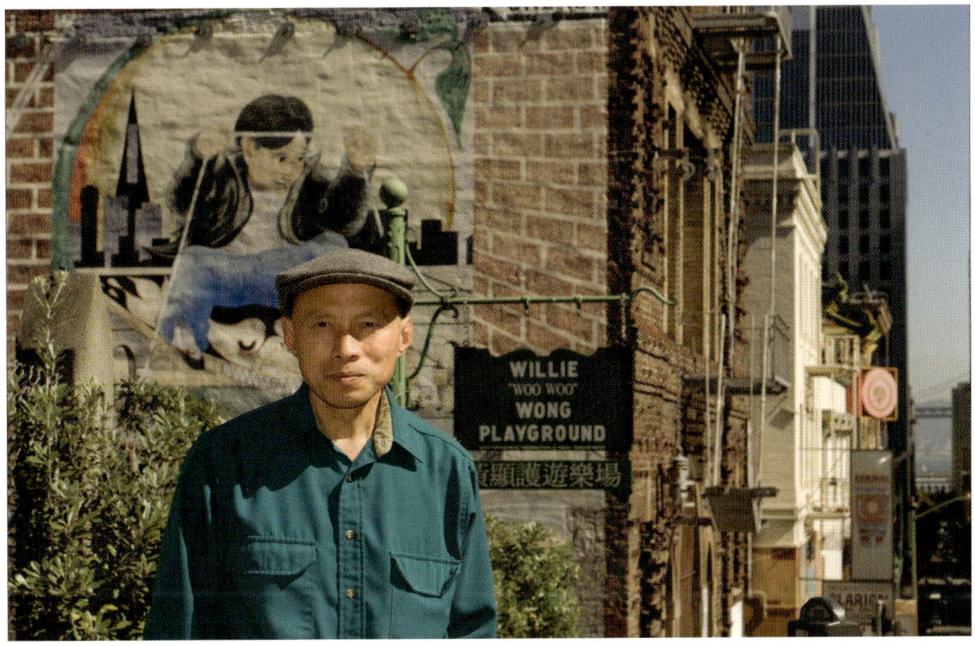

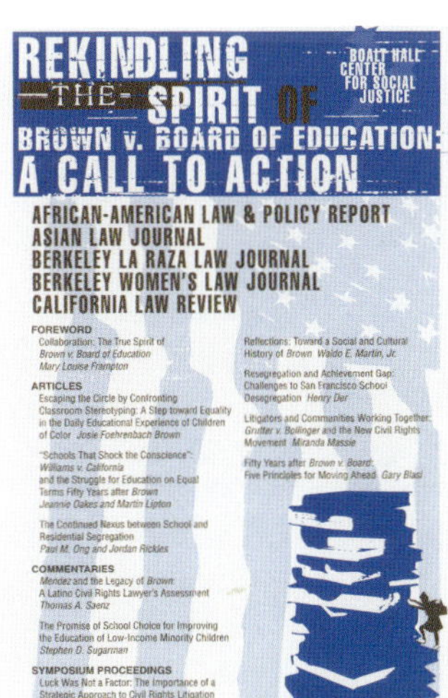

Henry Der
Community Activist
<u>Artifact</u>: "Rekindling the Spirit" flier
Boalt Hall Center for Social Justice, 2004
Henry has been analyzing the San Francisco public school system's racial imbalances and its de facto re-segregation.

Donna Keiko Ozawa

A photograph in the Kearny Street Workshop archives inspired *Robbie was there I* and *II*. The photograph, taken by Calvin Roberts — aka "Robbie," an early KSW artist/activist who was then vice chair of the Tenants Association — shows Sheriff Richard Hongisto using a sledgehammer on a door during the forceful eviction of the International Hotel (the original location of KSW) in August of 1977 (See page 29). Hongisto had originally refused to carry out the eviction order, earning himself five days in jail for contempt; he finally relented, and, moments before this photograph was taken Roberts recalls hearing him say, "Give me that hammer. Let me have a go at that. All I do is sit at a desk all day."

In 1977, I was only fourteen years old and did not realize the full significance of the I-Hotel events. But seeing this photo conjured up my own memories of 1992, when my partner Indigo and I were arrested on the orders of the same Richard Hongisto, by that time the chief of police under Mayor Frank Jordan. Indigo and I were part of a large, peaceful demonstration protesting the "not guilty" verdict in the case of the LAPD officers who had been caught on videotape brutally beating African American motorist, Rodney King. (The incident later became the subject of my sculpture, *The Beating,* pictured on page 27.) Hongisto ordered that all protesters on Market Street be rounded up. Indigo and I happened to be marching with a group of Asian Americans; Hongisto had the Asian American cops cuff us. The plastic cable ties on my wrists were so tight they nearly cut off all circulation and left their marks for two weeks. Hundreds of us were taken away in paddy wagons and held for hours in a warehouse (which smelled like cow manure) before being released. Thanks to the San Francisco Lawyers Guild, all of us sued the City and won $800 each. Indigo and I bought new Mac computers that facilitated our artwork for years.

When I saw Robbie's photo, I wondered about how it felt to be that close to Richard Hongisto when he took that first swing. Later, after recalling the early KSW days, Nancy Hom lamented that present day activists have no music — just crusty folk songs from the past that they don't know the words to. With this in mind, I made the sound for the door piece *Robbie was there, II:* absent-minded humming of "We Shall Not Be Moved," a protest song first popularized during the labor movement in the 1930s.

Many older KSW activists look at their history with nostalgia. Today, I see fatigued activists turning toward Buddhist meditation. *Weather Buddha* is one result of my ruminations on present day activism and spirituality, pop art and the aesthetic of displaying Asian antiquities and spiritual objects often on display at the Asian Art Museum, where I once worked as a mountmaker.

As a sculptor, I want to invite physical engagement in real time since our current culture virtualizes everything, creating an environment of sensory deprivation. For me, the hand crank has always been a symbol of our analog nature. (See *Crank Therapy* and *Help I*.) In *Sheep house,* as the viewer turns a hand-activated crank, a house rotates and the muffled sound of a sheep emerges from the window. This seemingly cheerful piece continues my critical examination of the American ideal of success and happiness, the pursuit of which is often mistakenly viewed as separate from politics, yet sacrifices our humanity and freedom.

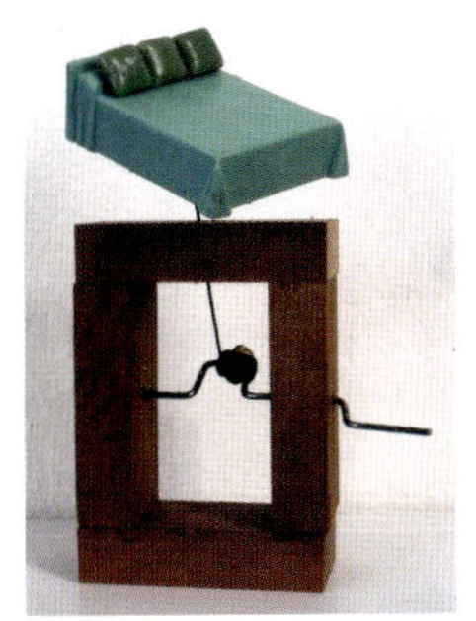

CRANK THERAPY
2003
wood, wire, plastic,
green gum and hot glue
6 x 5 x 3 in.
(photo by Sibila Savage)

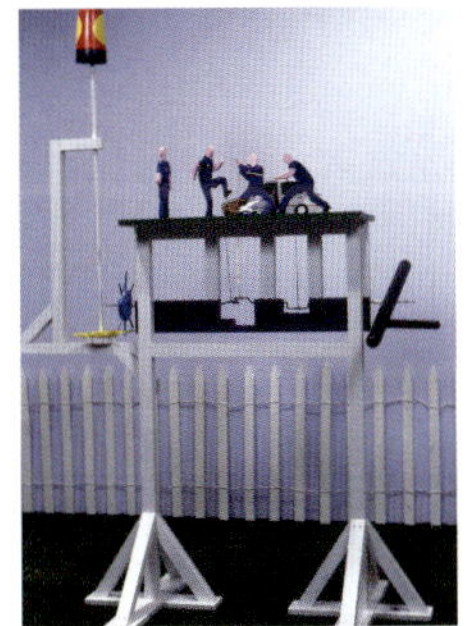

THE BEATING
1997
wood, steel, paint,
and nylon
6 x 3 x 2 ft., figures: 8 in.
the entire installation,
22 x 12 x 6 ft.
(photo by James Prinz)

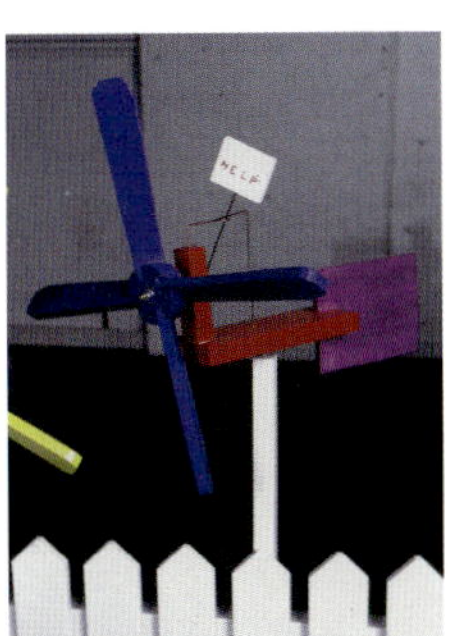

HELP I
1999
wood, steel, paint,
beads, brass, picket fence
12 x 12 x 11 in.
(photo by Catrina Marchetti)

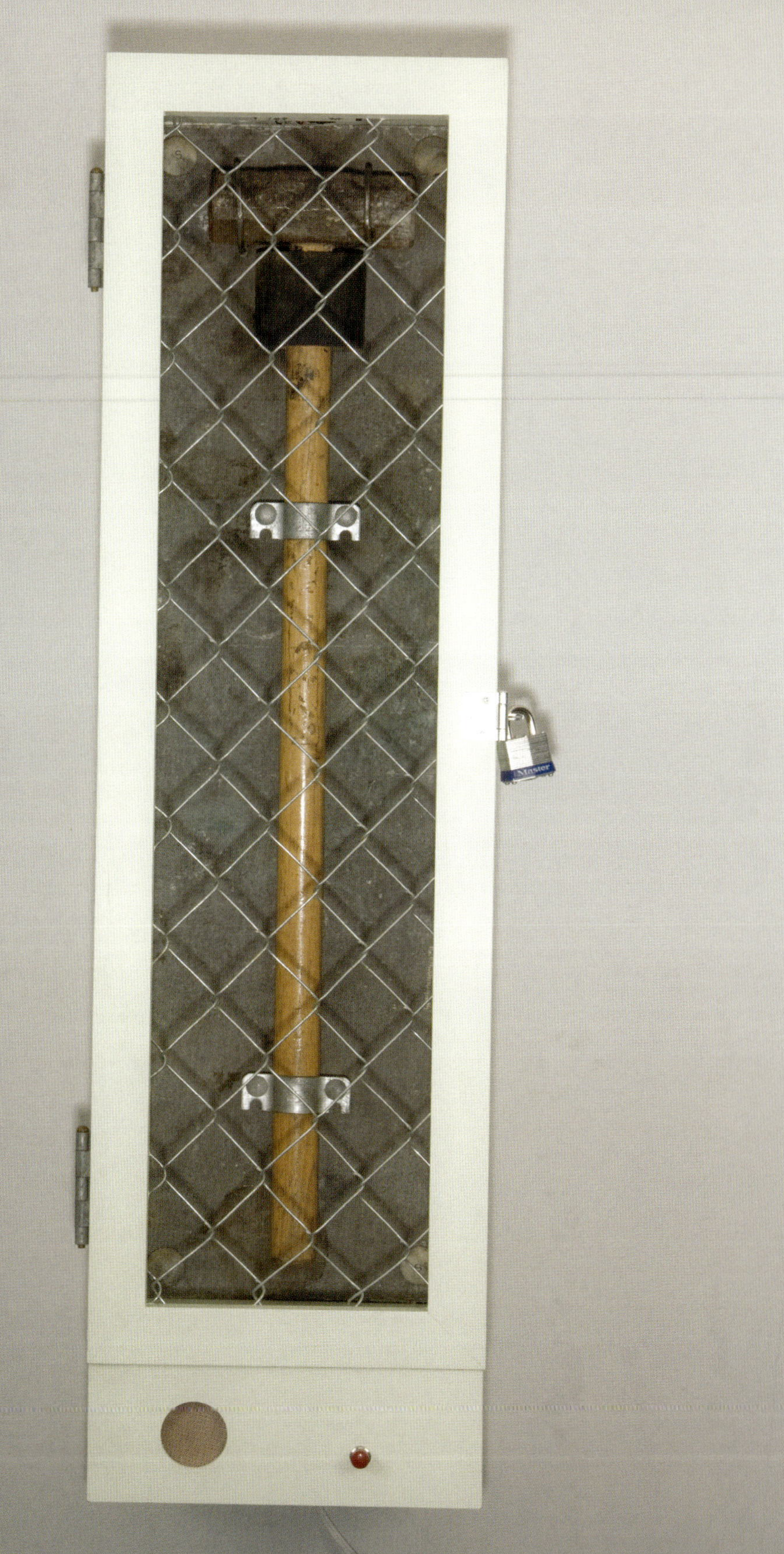

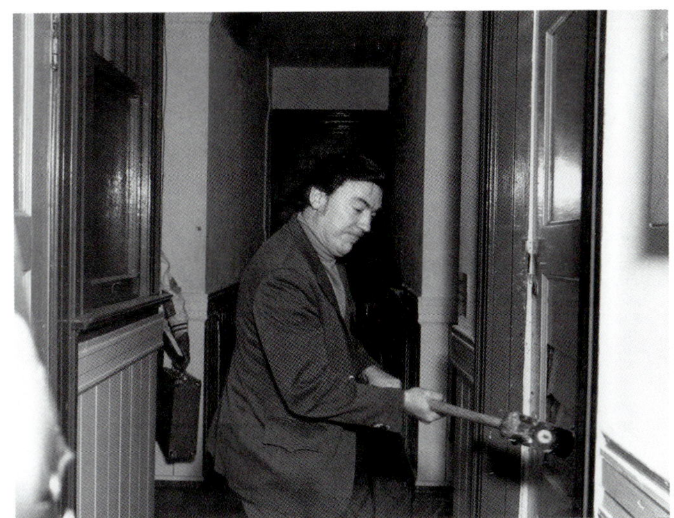

Photograph of Richard Hongisto
taken by Calvin "Robbie" Roberts, 1977

ROBBIE WAS THERE, I
2008
mixed media, electronics
12 x 44 x 10 in.
(photo by Bob Hsiang)

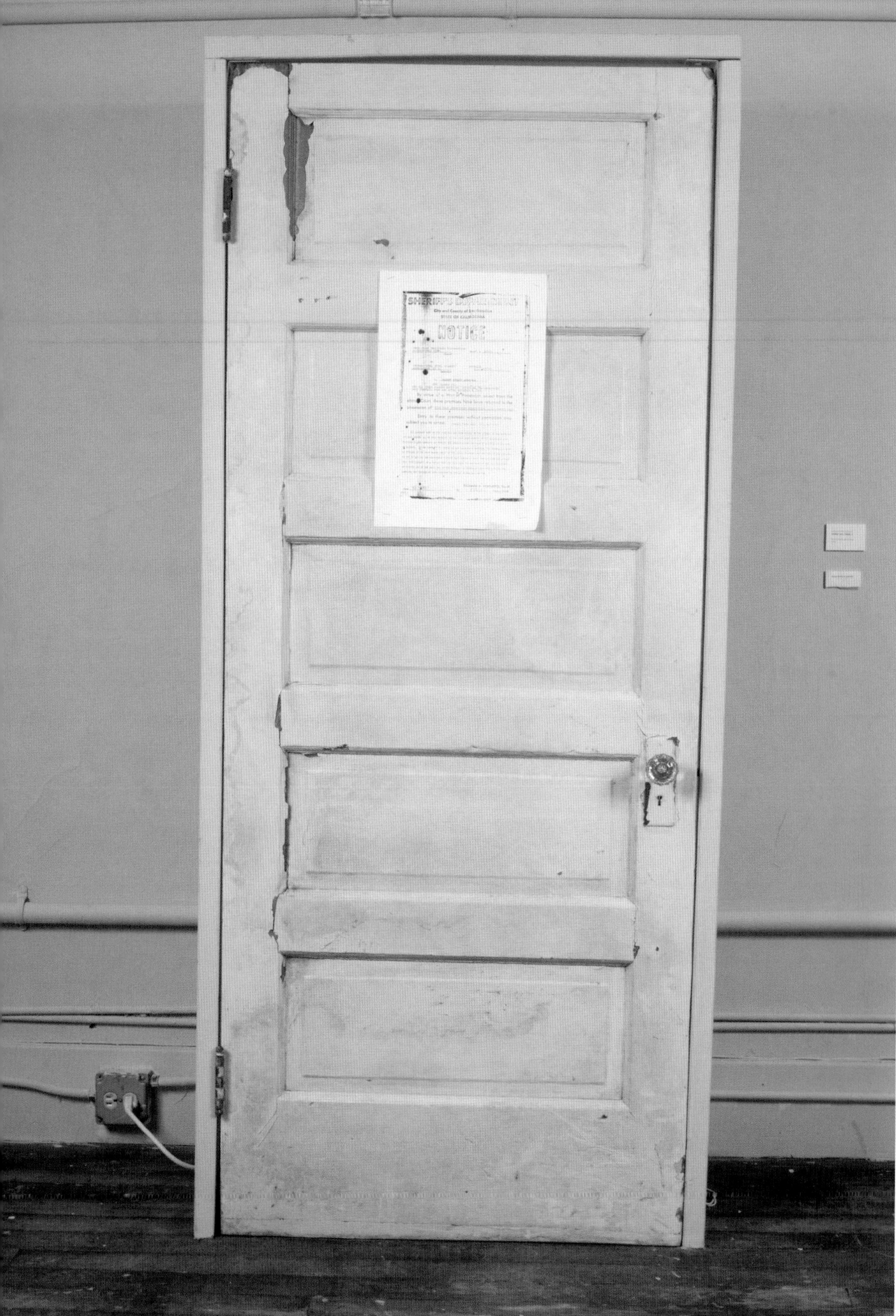
SHERIFF'S DEPARTMENT
City and County of San Francisco
STATE OF CALIFORNIA
NOTICE

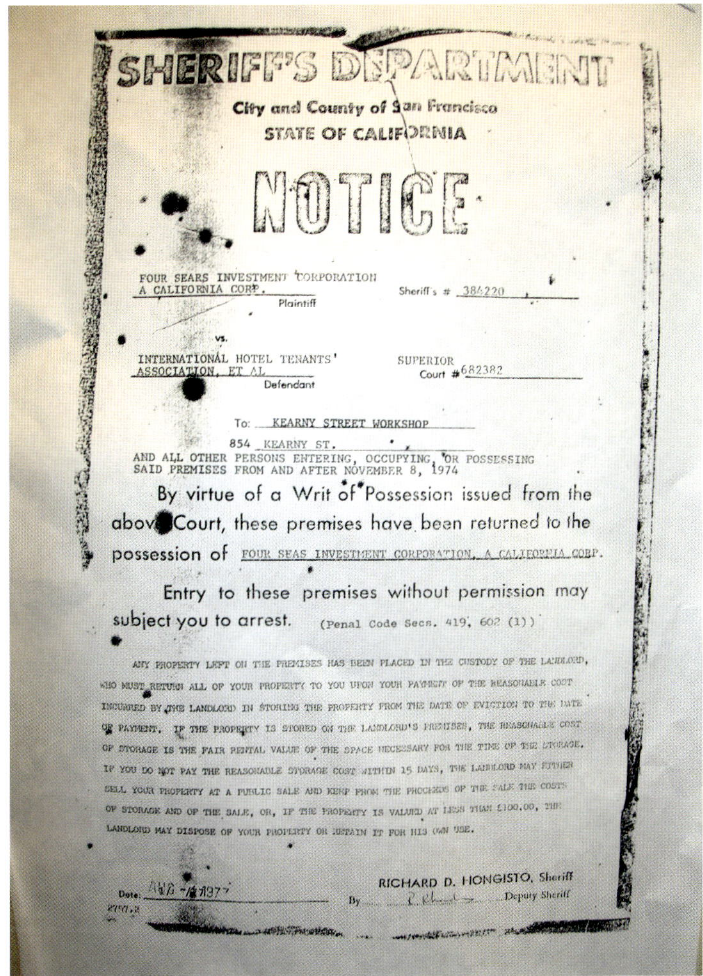

SHERIFF'S DEPARTMENT
City and County of San Francisco
STATE OF CALIFORNIA

NOTICE

FOUR SEARS INVESTMENT CORPORATION
A CALIFORNIA CORP.
                                    Sheriff's # 384220
        Plaintiff

vs.

INTERNATIONAL HOTEL TENANTS'   SUPERIOR
ASSOCIATION, ET AL   Court # 682382
        Defendant

To: KEARNY STREET WORKSHOP

     854 KEARNY ST.
AND ALL OTHER PERSONS ENTERING, OCCUPYING, OR POSSESSING
SAID PREMISES FROM AND AFTER NOVEMBER 8, 1974

By virtue of a Writ of Possession issued from the above Court, these premises have been returned to the possession of FOUR SEAS INVESTMENT CORPORATION, A CALIFORNIA CORP.

Entry to these premises without permission may subject you to arrest.   (Penal Code Secs. 419, 602 (1))

ANY PROPERTY LEFT ON THE PREMISES HAS BEEN PLACED IN THE CUSTODY OF THE LANDLORD, WHO MUST RETURN ALL OF YOUR PROPERTY TO YOU UPON YOUR PAYMENT OF THE REASONABLE COST INCURRED BY THE LANDLORD IN STORING THE PROPERTY FROM THE DATE OF EVICTION TO THE DATE OF PAYMENT. IF THE PROPERTY IS STORED ON THE LANDLORD'S PREMISES, THE REASONABLE COST OF STORAGE IS THE FAIR RENTAL VALUE OF THE SPACE NECESSARY FOR THE TIME OF THE STORAGE. IF YOU DO NOT PAY THE REASONABLE STORAGE COST WITHIN 15 DAYS, THE LANDLORD MAY EITHER SELL YOUR PROPERTY AT A PUBLIC SALE AND KEEP FROM THE PROCEEDS OF THE SALE THE COSTS OF STORAGE AND OF THE SALE, OR, IF THE PROPERTY IS VALUED AT LESS THAN $100.00, THE LANDLORD MAY DISPOSE OF YOUR PROPERTY OR RETAIN IT FOR HIS OWN USE.

Date: AUG -1 1977   RICHARD D. HONGISTO, Sheriff
2757.2   By   Deputy Sheriff

Detail to *Robbie was there, II*
a photocopy of the original eviction notice served to
Kearny Street Workshop at the original International Hotel.
Courtesy of KSW archives, 1977

LEFT:
ROBBIE WAS THERE, II
2008
mixed media, electronics
35 x 81 x 21 in.
(photo by Bob Hsiang)

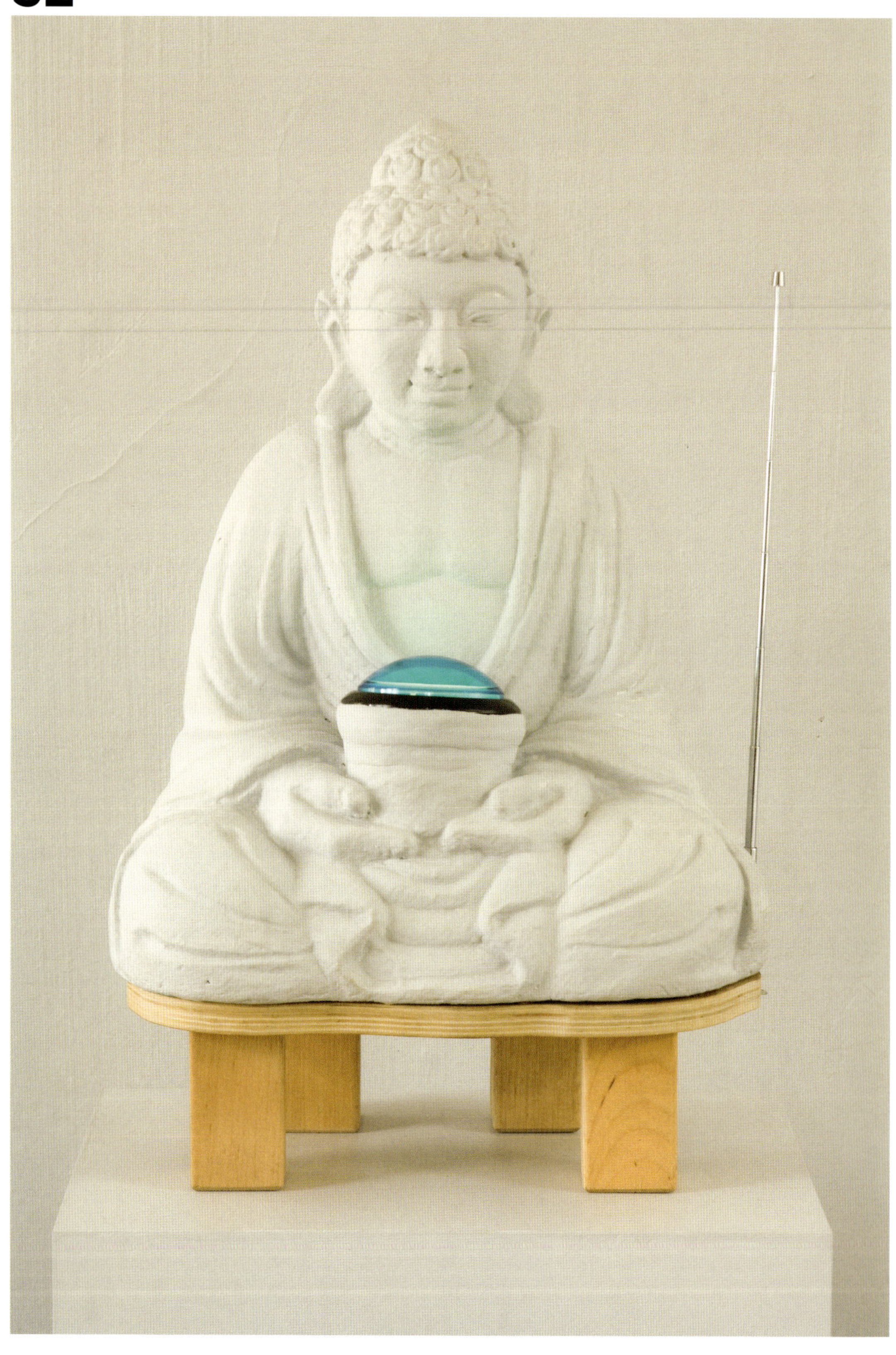

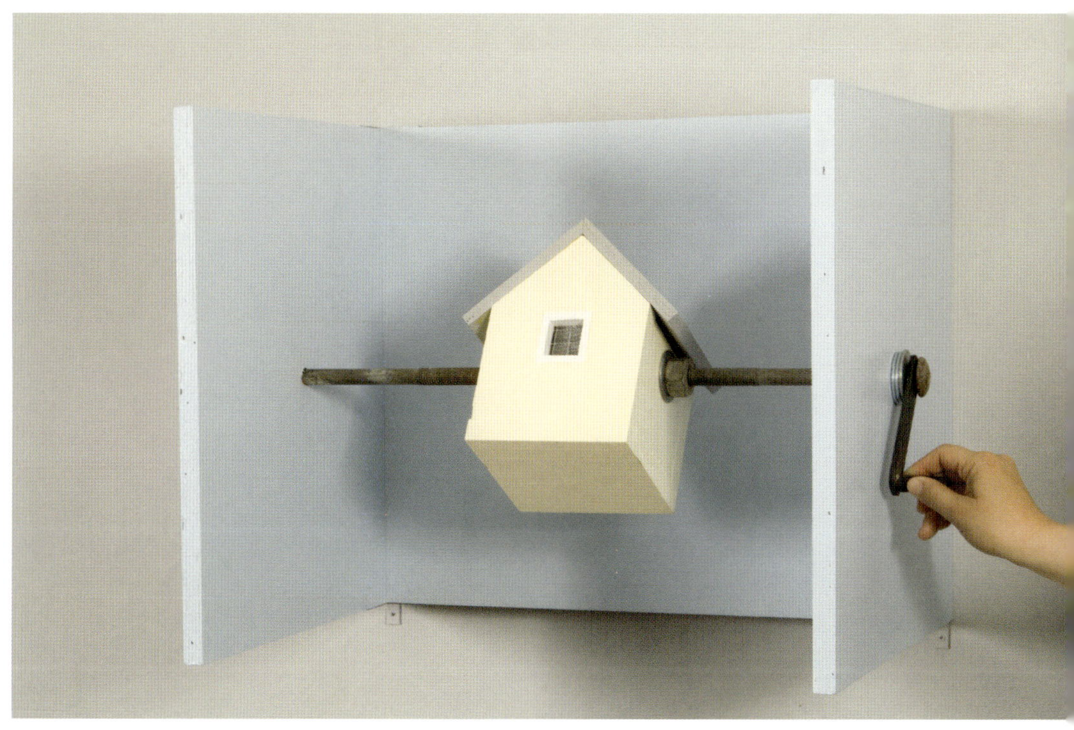

SHEEP HOUSE I
2008
mixed media, noisemaker
22 x 18 x 16 in.
(photo by Bob Hsiang)

WEATHER BUDDHA
2008
mixed media, electronics
13 x 24 x 10 in.
(photo by Bob Hsiang)

Christine Wong Yap

My work is defined by my ambivalence between optimism and pessimism. I see pessimism as rooted in the quotidian, while optimism correlates to transcendence. Analogously, art must be materialized, and yet art is still expected, quite optimistically, to convey the ineffable, or to illuminate the unknown.

Rather than investigating activism-as-subject, I took *Activist Imagination* as an opportunity to consider how participation in activism is shaped by fundamental views of how one sees the world and one's reflection in the world. Whether one's views or actions can have an impact on the world — indeed, on the future of activism — is essentially a negotiation between optimism and pessimism. I decided to pursue works that offer opportunities for viewers to either enact or consider their own agency.

My contributions share the theme of perception—highlighting the lens through which one sees the world—as well as my assumptions that optimism is happy, bright, vulnerable, rare, clear, and pessimism is unhappy, dark, powerful, abundant and distorted.

The curatorial project is intended to acknowledge KSW's graphic legacy as well as my sense of chronological distance from the conditions in which KSW emerged. While KSW's political activities may be well known, I sought to inject some original style and funk, underscored with informal exhibition strategies.

The Best Person I Can Be is a two-part interactive installation offering opportunities for reflection that are vulnerably optimistic (What does the best person I can be look like?) and safely pessimistic (an anti-social space for scrutiny). The installation attempts to make physical the act of seeing oneself reflected in other people.

Anyone can shape the future of activism. Participation will be informed by one's view of the world at large. An untitled window intervention functions to illustrate views of the world. Rose-colored lenses puncture a dominant, darkened view. Less common are views to see the world clearly.

Seeing Red is an edition of screen-printed glasses with lenses of Rubylith, a two-part film used in screen-printing. Anger can be motivating, but emotional extremes — like activism fueled by moral outrage and unchecked by political rigor — can be counterproductive. *Seeing Red* is a proposal for lenses to be worn and removed.

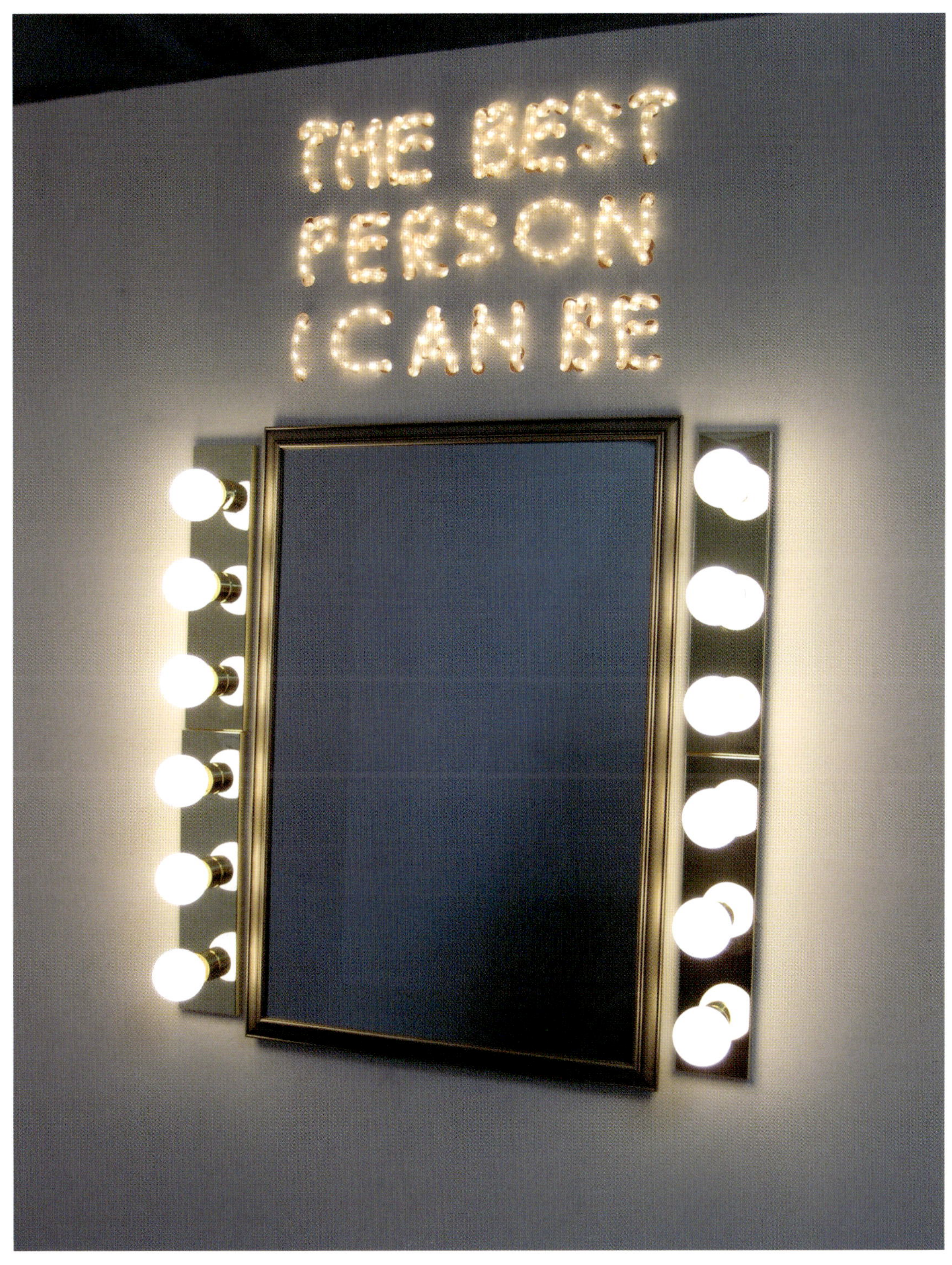
THE BEST
PERSON
I CAN BE

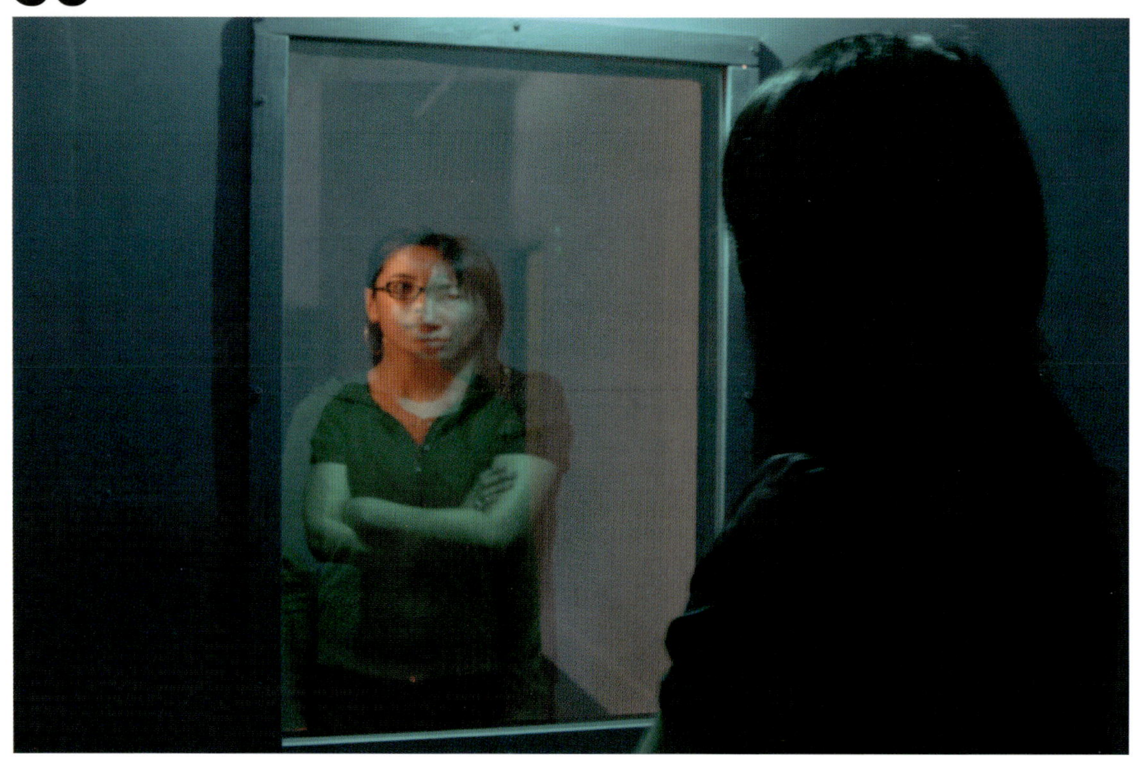

THE BEST PERSON I CAN BE
2008
installation, 8 x 8 x 8 ft.
(photo, page 35, by Christine Wong Yap
photo, this page, by Bob Hsiang)

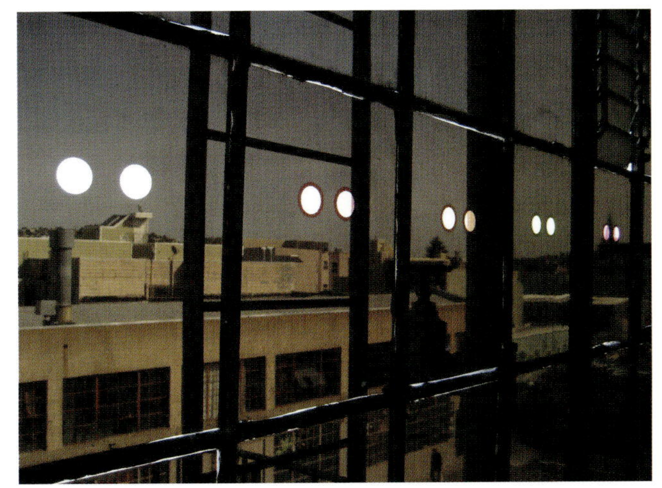

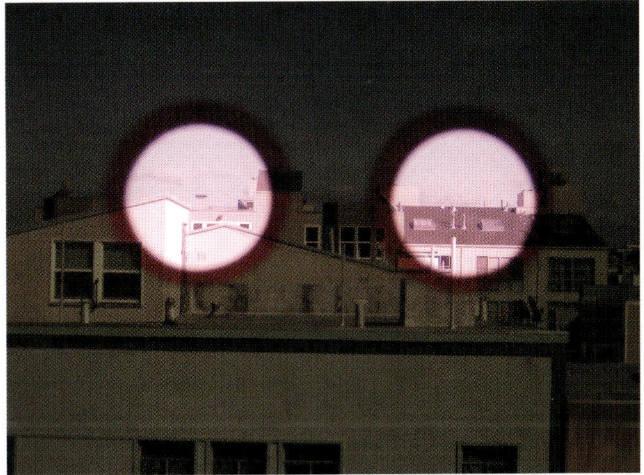

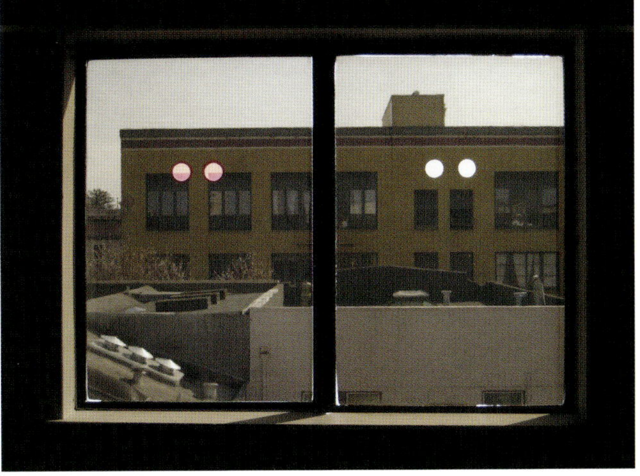

UNTITLED
2008
site-specific window intervention:
window tint, gels, tape, 9 x 7 ft. / 4 x 3 ft.
(photos by Christine Wong Yap)

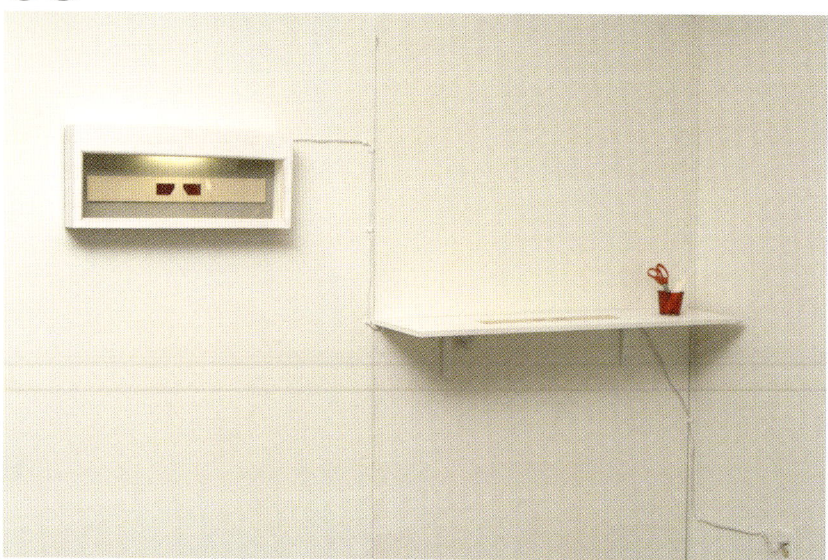

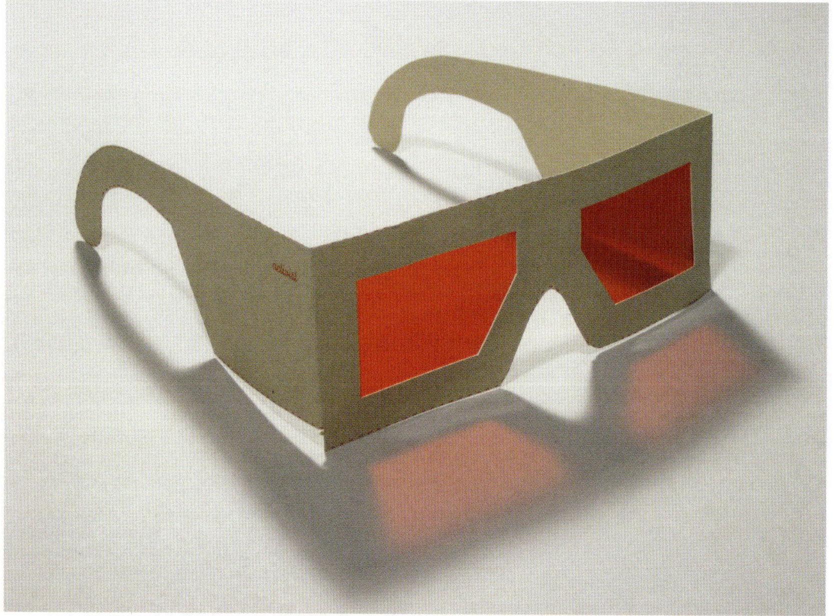

SEEING RED
2008
lightbox, limited edition multiple, shelf, tools,
8 x 6 x 1 ft.
(top photo, installation, by Bob Hsiang,
bottom photo, detail of glasses cut out by viewer,
by Christine Wong Yap)

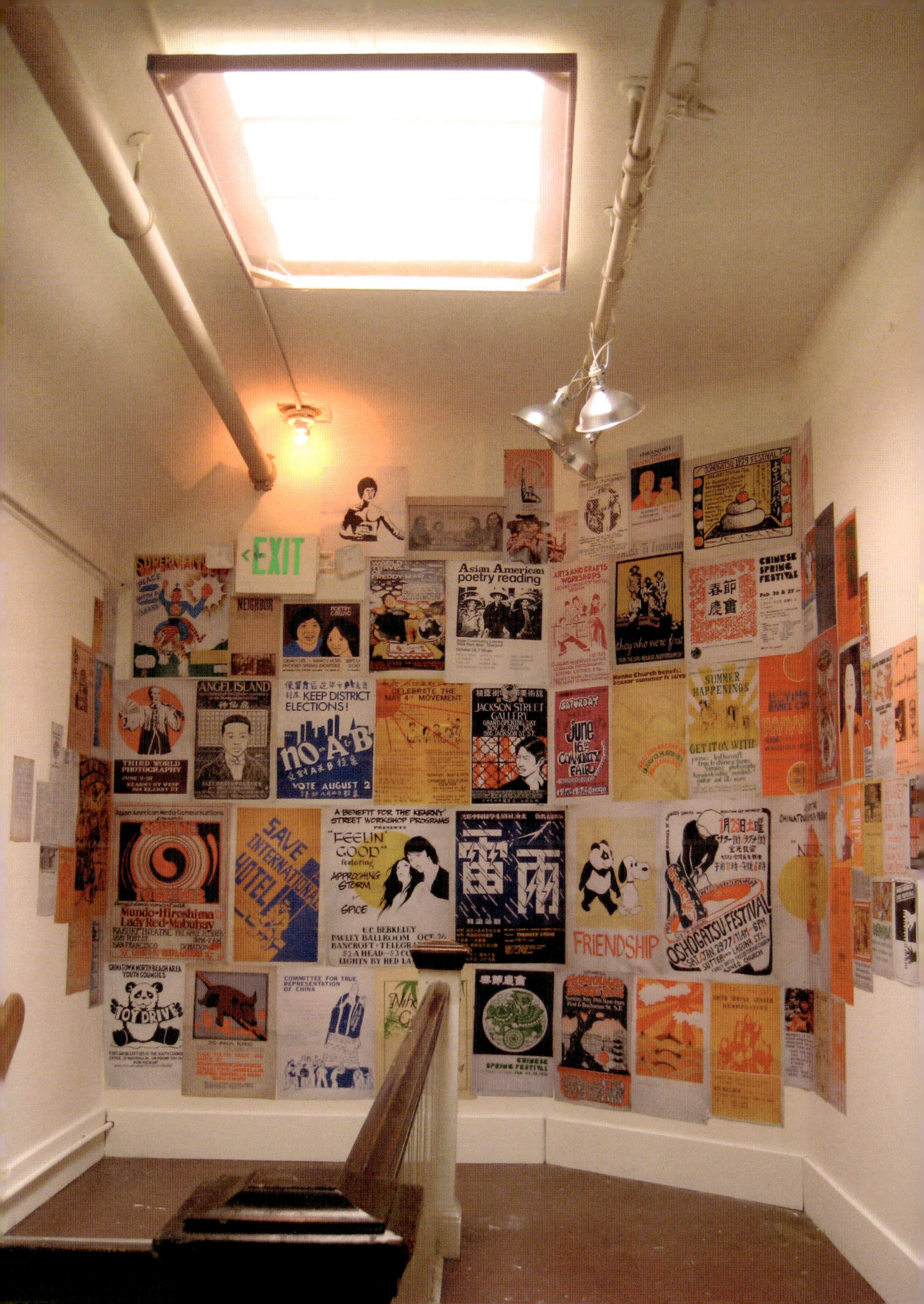

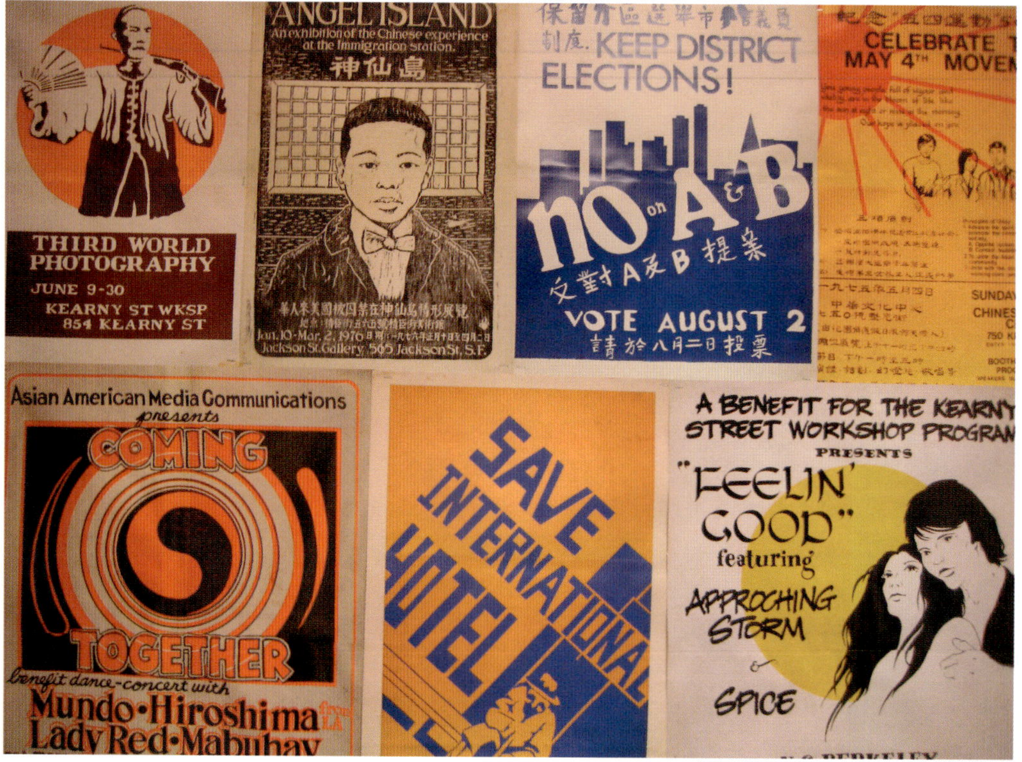

**EXHIBITION OF REPRODUCTIONS OF
KEARNY STREET WORKSHOP POSTERS,
CURATED BY CHRISTINE WONG YAP**
Kearny Street Workshop artists,
including Zand Gee, Nancy Hom, Jack Loo, Mitsui
Murai, Leland Wong and others
1974–1983
digital prints, 10 x 10 x 10 ft.
(photos by Christine Wong Yap)

41
DISCUSSION SERIES

November 27, 2007

THE JOURNEY SO FAR: 35 YEARS OF ACTIVISM

A discussion with Nancy Hom, Oscar Peñaranda, and Min Paek about the past three and a half decades of activism, the arts, and community.

Moderated by Alison Lee Satake

Co-presented with the International Hotel Manilatown Center and the Manilatown Heritage Foundation.

Tuesday, January 22 , 2008

WHERE WE ARE NOW: ACTIVISM TODAY

A discussion with Eric Mar, Diana Pei Wu, Favianna Rodriguez, and Le Tim Ly about the present state of activism, the arts and community.

Moderated by Robynn Takayama

Thursday, March 27, 2008

WHERE WE ARE GOING: THE FUTURE OF ACTIVISM

A discussion with Ron Muriera, Erika Chong Shuch, Pireeni Sundaralingam, and Carlos Villa about the future of activism, the arts and community.

Moderated by Wei Ming Dariotis

Thursday, April 24, 2008

ARTIST TALK

A discussion about the exhibition with lead artists Bob Hsiang, Donna Keiko Ozawa, and Christine Wong Yap.

Moderated by Samantha Chanse

THE ACTIVIST IMAGINATION BLOG (ONGOING)

A cyber-discussion about the *Activist Imagination* program and about activism, the arts, and community.

http://kearnystreet.wordpress.com/category/activist-imagination/

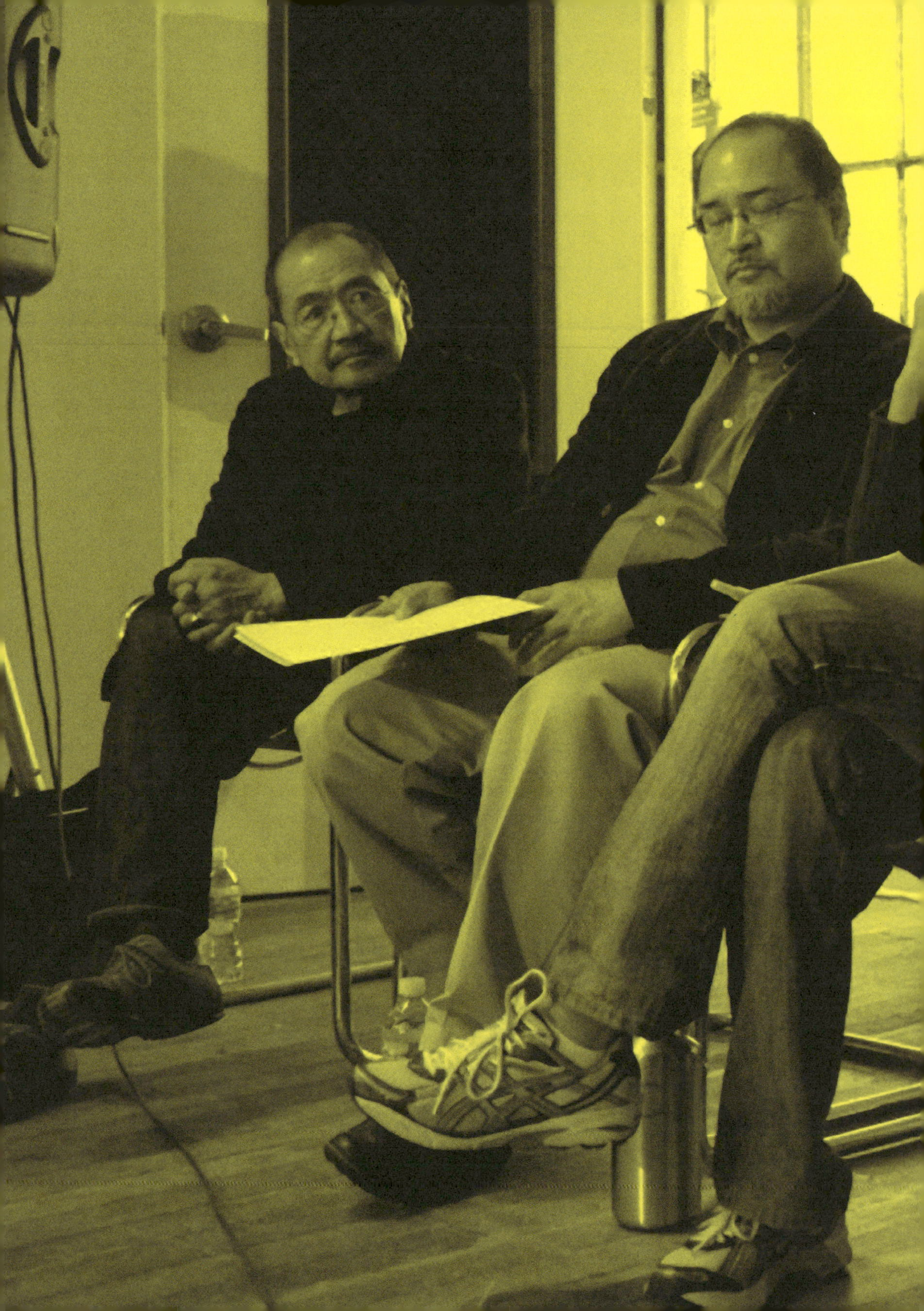

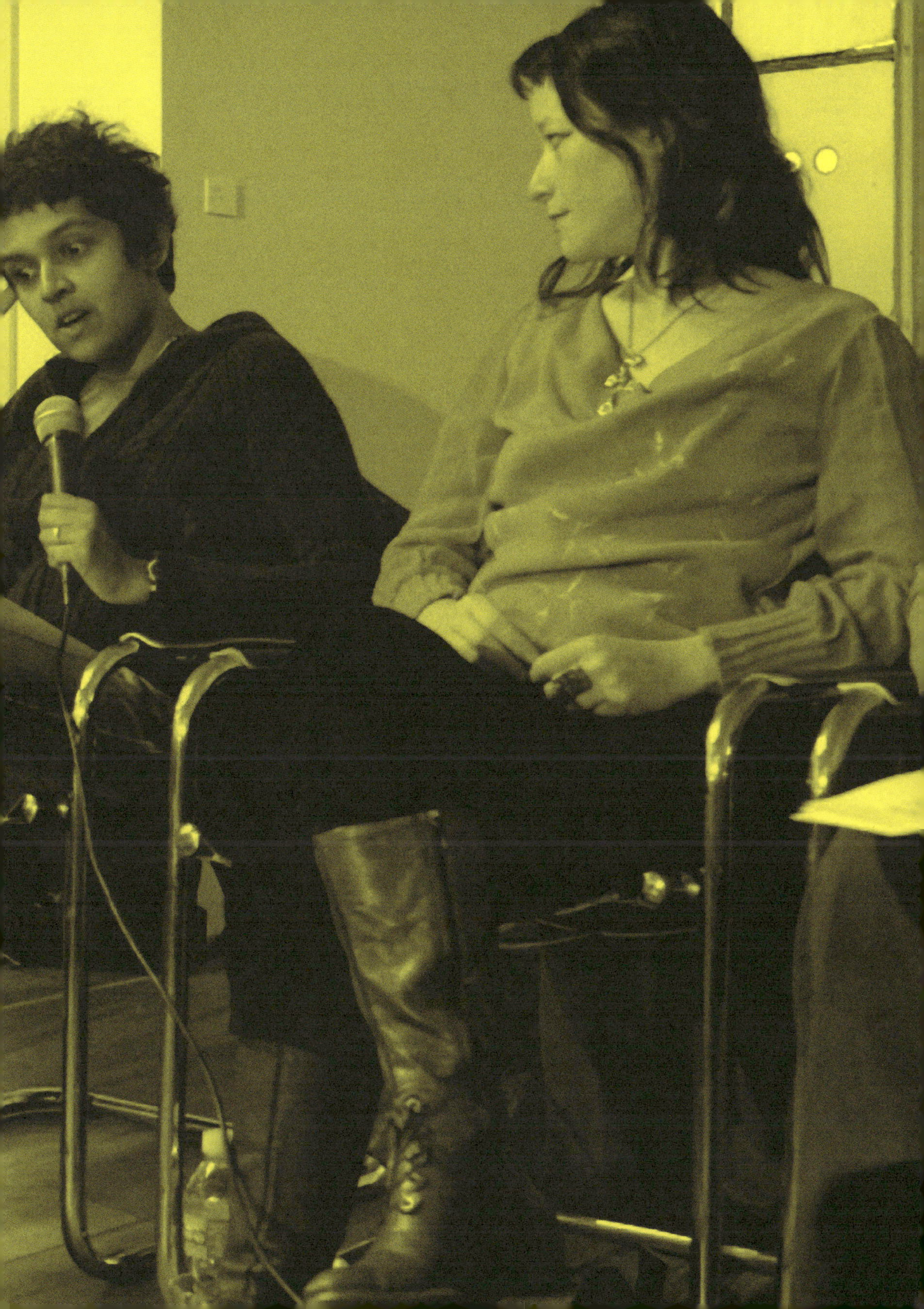

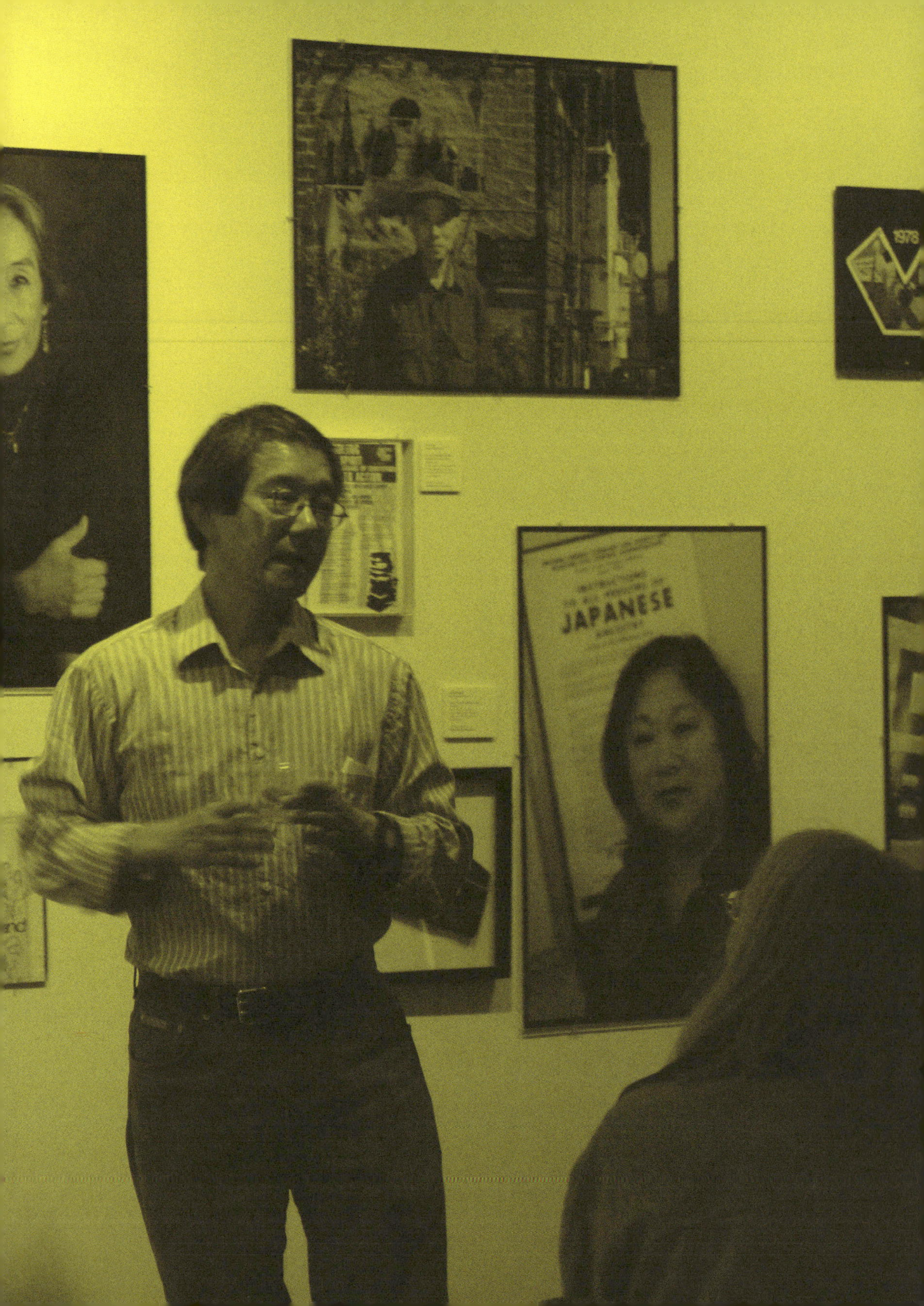

1978
JAPANESE

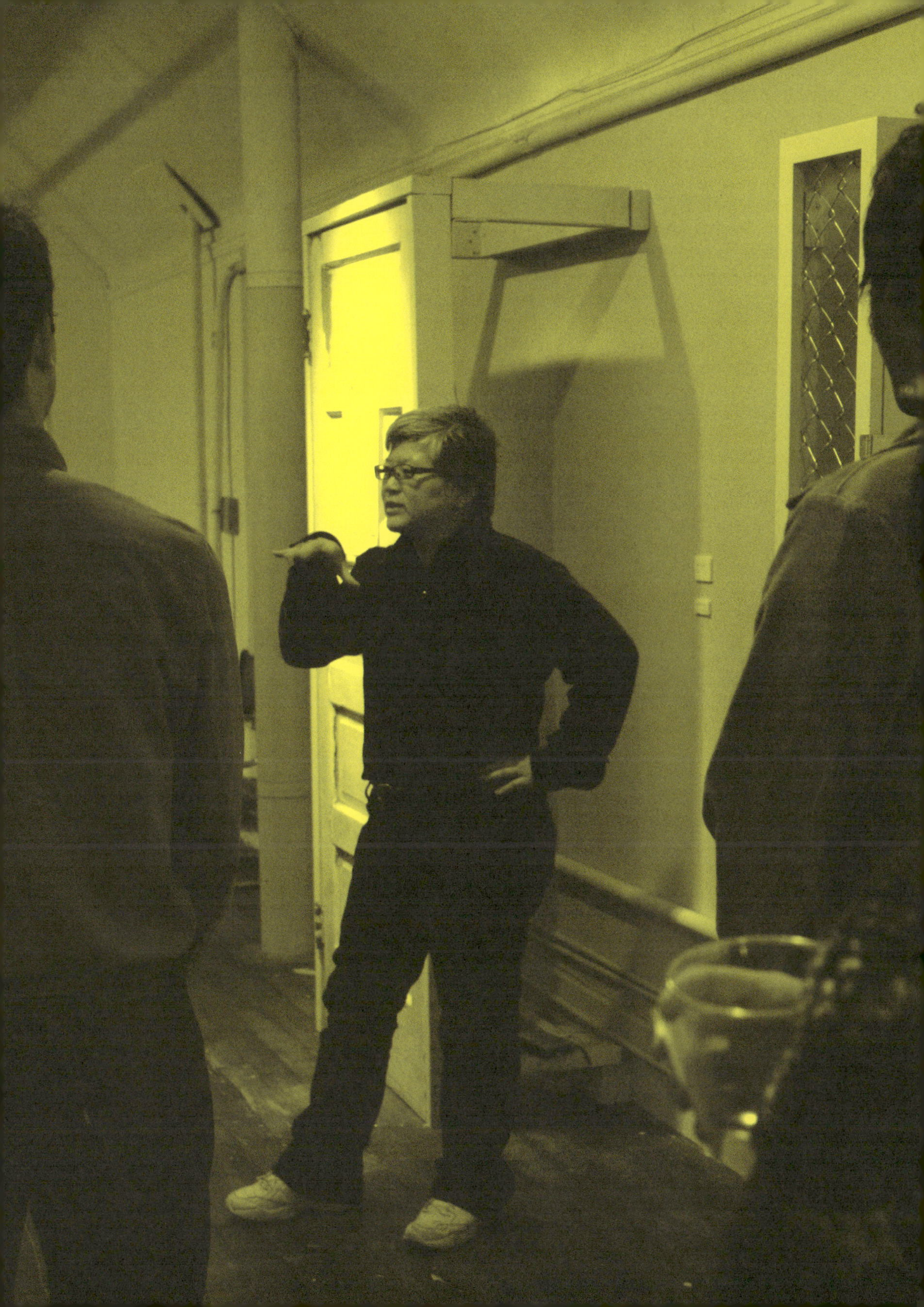

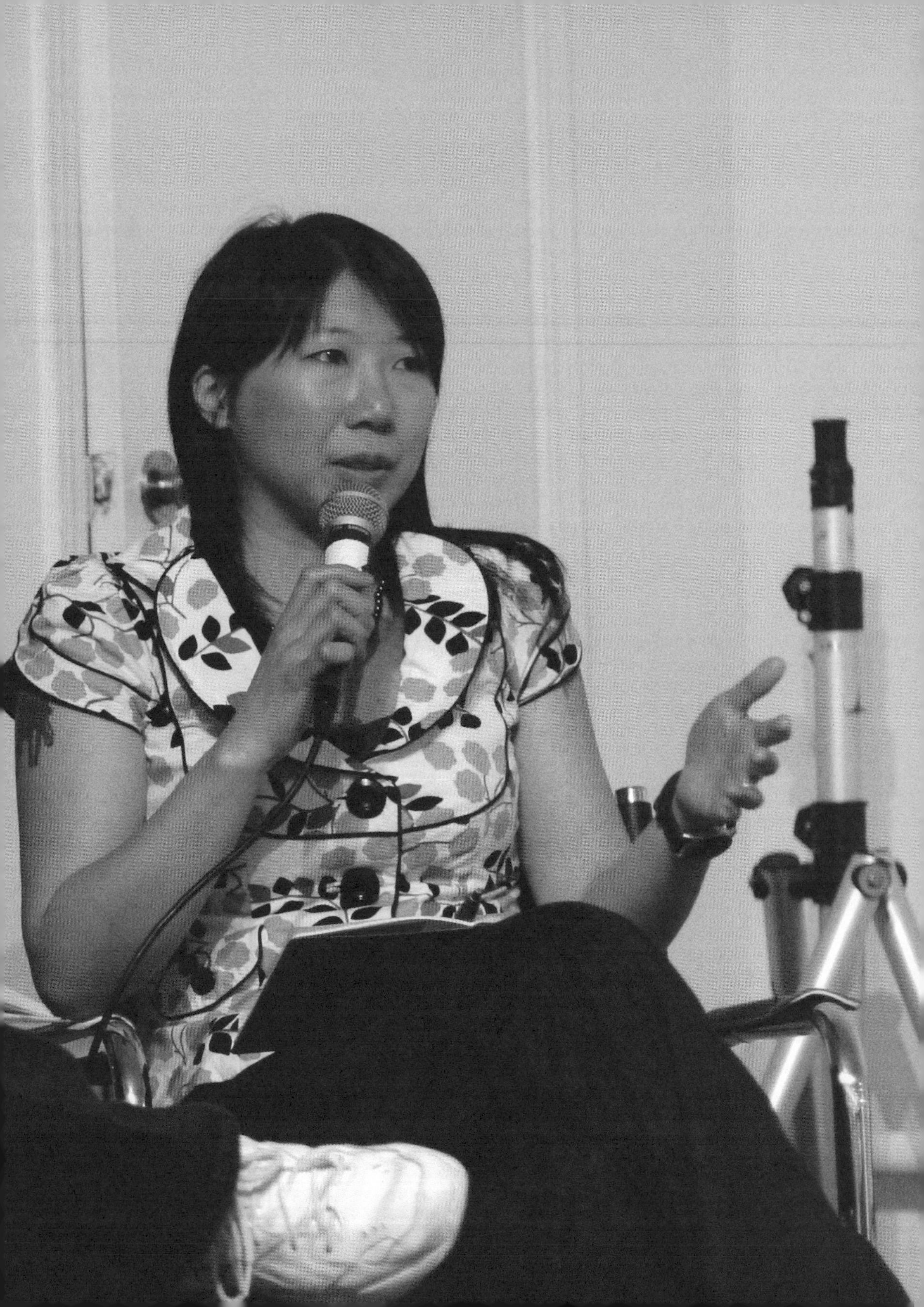

As part of the *Activist Imagination project,* KSW presented a series of discussions exploring the past, present, and future of activism, the arts, and APA communities. This series took place November 27, 2007 through April 24, 2008, and featured prominent artists and activists based in the San Francisco Bay Area.

The first discussion, *The Journey So Far: 35 years of activism,* took place November 27, 2007, at the International Hotel Manilatown Center, and was co-presented by the Manilatown Heritage Foundation. The panel featured Nancy Hom, Min Paek, and Oscar Peñaranda, and was moderated by Alison Lee Satake.

The second discussion, *Where Are We Now: activism today,* took place January 22, 2008, at KSW's space180, and featured panelists Le Tim Ly, Eric Mar, Favianna Rodriguez, and Diana Pei Wu. The panel was moderated by Robynn Takayama.

The third discussion, *Where Are We Going: the future of activism,* took place March 27, 2008, at KSW's space180, with panelists Ron Muriera, Erika Chong Shuch, Pireeni Sundaralingam, and Carlos Villa, and was moderated by Wei Ming Dariotis.

On April 24, 2008, our discussion series concluded with the *Activist Imagination* artist talk, with Bob Hsiang, Donna Keiko Ozawa, and Christine Wong Yap.

Below are selected excerpts from the conversations that took place during this discussion series.

NOVEMBER 27, 2007
The Journey So Far: 35 years of activism.
Discussion with Nancy Hom, artist, writer, curator, KSW advisory board member, and KSW executive director 1995 - 2003; Oscar Peñaranda, educator, writer, and community activist; and Min Paek, founder and executive director of the Korean American Women Artists and Writers Association. Moderated by Alison Lee Satake, journalist and writer.

EXCERPTS FROM DISCUSSION:

Oscar Peñaranda:…I remember we had to do a lot of painting and repair work in the basement [at the original Kearny Street Workshop], so…[laughs]…I really didn't look forward to coming into the building. But once I got there I met some great people and I remember Jim Dong and his wife Gail at the time…Lou Syquia, other writers and artists, Al Robles, of course…I didn't know it would last this long, I didn't know it was an organization that was going to be a driving force for many other artists and activists, but I'm glad I was part of it.

. . .

Nancy Hom: Many of our spontaneous ideas at Kearny Street Workshop came up at bars and restaurants, where we gathered after the meetings. At one of those occasions we just talked about doing a film, "Yeah we should do a film," — "Yeah let's do a film!" — "Oh, how about something significant like, McDonald's versus *dim sum?*" — "Yeah, let's do that!" And the very next day we bought McDonald's hamburgers, French fries, whatever, and we got some dim sum, and I had my Super 8 camera, and we actually animated an entire battle scene, with armies of French fries and one-on-one combat between hot dogs and *char siu baos.* There was total destruction at the end, ketchup covering everything. We went to Jackson Street Gallery on a Friday night, and we didn't leave until Sunday morning. By that time, it looked really gross; we even filmed a cockroach crawling along the set, a perfect symbol for the futility of war. But the reason why I remember anecdotes like this so much is that nothing stopped us. It was just the pure joy of creating something together, on the spur of the moment, and it just didn't matter if we had money or the resources or even a story line, we just went and did it. Some of the stuff we created ended up in the garbage can, but a lot of that stuff created the impetus for us to do what is known as more serious work. That spirit stayed with us. At least it stayed with me for thirty-three years, and I can tell it to you as one of my cherished memories.

. . .

Alison Lee Satake: What do you think is the strongest motivation for political action?

Oscar Peñaranda: I don't think it's a single thing or a couple of things, I think it's the explosion of the whole thing. We really didn't have to wait to be politicized, we had no choice. There were so many things happening around our lives and we couldn't escape the heaviness of the politics at the time — the politics were being shoved down your throat. …As artists…you learned to answer back or fight back to reflect the reality of the times. So if you say was it one thing or another thing in my life, it was many things. My friends were all going to Vietnam, I was going to school but the school that I went to had a hundred cops, two hundred cops, they had rifles, they had dogs, they had tanks, you know — In the schools. They had barbed wire, our president was turning against us, it was crazy everywhere I went. I worked a part-time job, the older folks were telling me, "What are you guys doing? You're destroying everything! What kind of plan do you have for society if it's all crazy like this?" The gap was there everywhere we went.

Nancy Hom: I went to Pratt Institute in New York, which is the equivalent of San Francisco Art Institute — very fine art-oriented. But even when I was going to school I couldn't help but be in the turmoil of the times because the turmoil came to the school. Pratt Institute was a mostly white school surrounded by a poor black community, so you knew there was going to be a lot of consciousness-raising there. I had an interest in journalism so I joined a newspaper at the school that came out every week without fail. I did everything at the newspaper pretty much the way I work with organizations now. Besides feature writing, one of my jobs was covering the news, which was very exciting in the late '60s. I covered the Vietnam war protests and I found out about what was going on inside the school system. I protested perceived conservatism in the college and took over the dean's office. The turning point of consciousness for me — I remember very clearly because it was such an epiphany — was when I was watching TV and saw all these bombs and the voiceover was saying "We now declare war against Cambodia." To me that was the last straw; we were invading yet another country. And we don't have much of this in the media now, but at that time the media would show all these body bags coming home and all the bombs raining down on people and you could see very graphically what was going on. I saw the body bags and I watched them interview people in the villages that were being bombed and I saw that the people looked just like me. So here I was in an all-white school doing my little artwork and covering all these incredible news stories and seeing the bombing of Cambodia on TV. From then on I hardly finished any of my classes. I cut my classes and went to a lot of demonstrations because I felt I could not do what I normally did and also watch what was going on to people that looked like me. That became the start of this whole identity consciousness. It wasn't just about people on TV who looked like me, but I started noticing other people in my city who looked like me, and I started looking at my parents differently, wondering how they suffered where they came from, what oppressions occurred in their home countries, et cetera. So began a whole consciousness raising exploration, but it started with that TV program.

Alison Lee Satake: Sometimes I hear from young people today, "well this is wrong, I don't believe in this, but how can we possibly stop it?" Did that ever go through your mind at the time, during the Vietnam War?

Nancy Hom: That spirit I talked about earlier in conjunction with KSW is the same kind of spirit that gave us our optimism. It wasn't like "Oh, but I don't know how to stop it." It was more like "Oh, we gotta do something; let's do something." If you really thought about things too much maybe you would not do it — do you have the money, do you have the time, you got dishes to do, whatever it is you are thinking. A group from Pratt took over the Brooklyn Bridge one day and there were cops on the other end and people were preventing cars from going across the bridge. If we had really thought about it, it might have seemed like a stupid thing to do, but we didn't think too much about it. Like Oscar said, it didn't seem like we had a choice.

There's a lot to be cynical about the world; it hasn't changed that much and in many ways it's gotten worse. We need the things that used to spur us on; we need our songs, our speakers. Our songs used to be so important to us. We had "We are the Children" by Chris and Joanne but even mainstream songs, the Rolling Stones' "Streetfighting Man," for instance. I remember many protests with "Streetfighting Man." I went to an art school — they would blast it out into the streets with good speakers so you really marched to a tune. We had Bob Dylan, Joan Baez, Phil Ochs, and many others singing protest songs; we had the media working with us. It was not uncommon to turn on the tube and there's Norman Mailer; there's Abbie Hoffman telling you to go to steal the books right off the shelves. I feel like there's been a concentrated, well thought out cooption of the media and all the things that keep people together. People say we are more connected now with computers, but it is one person looking at a screen; it's not the same as having a song and marching together and feeling the energy from each other. That's why I'm very glad for gatherings like this. But that is the one difference that I see nowadays. We need intelligent, thought-provoking discussions and programs, uplifting songs and speeches that balance our cynicism.

. . .

Oscar Peñaranda: To me, activism and being an artist is kind of the same; it comes from the same source, at least. I'm an artist, I'm a writer, I read what's written, I never see my people in it. That's the first thing, I get pissed off. I live my life, I see my people living their lives, they have all kinds of great stories, but stories no one knows about, because all the stories written are written by mainstream people…I turn on the television now, there are no Filipino Americans…. it's almost a hundred percent white folks' stories. We have Asian American stories too but we don't see them. The only time I see them is when I turn off [the television], and I see my own reflection, that's the only time I see Filipinos on the television. So things like that, that's where the art comes from, you get pissed off about a lot of stuff, and then you write. Although to keep the art fine and true to the art, you have to outlast the being pissed off. In other words, you can't be angry a hundred percent of the time. But it gives you an impetus. Anger is a good impetus. It's not always the right impetus but it's an impetus, it comes from the same source. But what you're doing is your art.

Being part of a movement and being an artist sometimes conflict because being part of a movement is sort of a rah-rah thing, and if you're an artist, you don't want to do the rah-rah things too much. Because you see a vision and you have to get to that vision. And you see everybody else doing slogans. I'm a writer who doesn't like slogans, it doesn't matter what slogan it is, it's just that I want to create something new and slogans are kind of trite to me. But I didn't know, in my immature mind, that they can serve different purposes. …But there is a certain conflict between a movement and an artist, and an artist has to come to terms with that conflict. I've never met an artist who's very comfortable being engulfed in a movement.

Nancy Hom: I think there's always a conflict between artists and what our role is in society…I came from an art school that had a biased way of defining art. Even in the funding world, some funders define art a certain way; it's so easy to be pigeon-holed as a fine artist or a community artist, or to look down on one or the other. It's easy to place some art over here and some over there and say it's better art. It's so easy to draw all these boundaries that keep artists separate from each other, or keep the genres separate from each other. In art school, when I started getting politicized, my art began to change. I was ostracized by some of the professors who had loved my art before, when it was very abstract and didn't really mean that much to anybody, except that it had some kind of *je ne sais quoi* kind of quality. I was young enough to be really hurt by that and I had a lot of self-doubt. "Am I going off in a whole other direction that's away from art?…Should I go back to *the* art or I'll never get into *the* museum?" I pondered that for a while until the Asian American movement took over, and as a person of color I felt like I had no choice but to be there. Thirty-three years later I've come to a place where I am comfortable with my path. I define an activist artist or a community artist as one whose work has something to say to the community, has some relationship to the community. Whether I'm curating shows, growing organizations from scratch, writing, designing images, whatever it is that I'm doing, there is always a spark of creativity. So when I say I'm a community artist it does not just mean I do those posters that you know me for, and it doesn't even mean that I do it for the Chinese community because I'm Chinese or because all my work has to talk about my mother or whatever it is, it's that the intent of the work is always the same: I always have a community to relate to. My art or writing is not finished unless it is presented to the community. My work does not have as much meaning if I hang it in the Museum of Modern Art and no one from my community sees it. That artwork is not finished. I've done some work that has hung there, but I've also taken that same artwork and shown it where the community I created it for can see it. Then it is complete.

…There's no need to be self-righteous about one kind of art or another. Otherwise you get too judgmental and judgment kills creativity. Right away you start censoring yourself, others start censoring you, and before you know it we're not talking to each other. Community art is all about community building, relationships, interaction. That term really has a lot of meaning. I know that through the years some people have shied away from identifying with community art. They don't want to be boxed in; they don't want to do *that* kind of art. I feel the opposite, that it opens the door to many connections and many ways of relating. The whole secret to it is to know who you are, what you stand for, what you're about, and then getting your work out to the community you intend to see it.

<u>**JANUARY 22, 2008**</u>
Where We Are Now: activism today.
Discussion with Le Tim Ly, activist and co-founder of Liberation Ink; Eric Mar, activist and San Francisco School Board member; Favianna Rodriguez, artist-activist and founding member of Eastside Arts Alliance; and Diana Pei Wu, organizer and then Program Director for the National Network for Immigrant and Refugee Rights. Moderated by Robynn Takayama, independent radio producer and KSW advisory board member.

EXCERPTS FROM DISCUSSION:

Robynn Takayama: When we hear from the panelists tonight, we see how the arts has become an integral part of social justice work. But some cultural workers back in the day have said that they were told to put down the guitar and get into the factory! They said they practiced their music in secret. How have you been able to integrate art making into your politics and livelihood?

Le Tim Ly: I think a key component of the relationship between art and activism is the part that art can play in helping imagine a different world. In a time where our hopes and dreams are constructed around what we are able to consume and possess, art — when coupled with political education and organized resistance — provides us with a means to envision a world that reflects a set of values based on love, compassion and cooperation. And art can be the source of inspiration and renewal, reminding us of what we are building towards.

. . .

51 DISCUSSION SERIES

Diana Pei Wu: Social change and social justice is not just about whether we can make more money, have access to middle class benefits, and participate in the decisions that affect our lives and our communities. It is also fundamentally about living with and enacting values of social justice, equality, decolonization. To do that, we have to undo the development of 500 years of colonialism, racism and capitalism, and the ways that our concepts of nation and rights are inherently gendered and often patriarchal and heterosexist. In order to effectively lay bare and begin to unravel those structures of thought and action, we must have actors and creators in political, economic, social, artistic, cultural and spiritual realms.

. . .

Robynn Takayama: Artists are one of the most powerful tools in a movement. They can convey the righteous message in a way no political speech can. Photographers like Bob Hsiang and Leland Wong, poster artists like Christine Wong Yap and Favianna Rodriguez, musicians like Francisco Herrera and Kiwi capture the spirit of the movement with a single image, a single stanza in a song.

MARCH 27, 2008
Where We Are Going: the future of activism.

Discussion with Carlos Villa, artist, curator, producer, and professor at San Francisco Art Institute; Pireeni Sundaralingam, poet, playwright, cogntive scientist, former professor of Cognitive Development; Erika Chong Shuch, choreographer, dancer, educator, and director of Erika Shuch Performance Project; and Ron Muriera , performing artist-activist and executive director of Manilatown Heritage Foundation. Moderated by Wei Ming Dariotis, assistant professor of Asian American studies at San Francisco State University and KSW advisory board member.

EXCERPTS FROM DISCUSSION:

Pireeni Sundaralingam: We all have to make a decision about whether or not we want to be an artist or an activist, and which one is true to you... An activist has a clear message and an artist may have room for ambiguity and may even court ambiguity —

. . .

Carlos Villa: Some of the best moments I think have ever happened in Asian American poetry came from an old friend - Al Robles. Al had started a class at the Kearny Street Workshop, he also worked upstairs in the I-Hotel ...he would write letters for these older *manongs,* and what they would state were dreams, what they would state were hopes, what was also underlined was a lot of failure; but at the same time there was something very alive. And Al being the conduit that he was, made those utterances an incredible poetry by using language that was known as "pidgin," that was truly not only hapa but mestizo — mongrel, hybrid — whatever you want to call it. But it was ours, and actually enflamed and inspired many younger poets like Oscar Peñaranda, the Syquia brothers, and this whole group of artists that found voice in and found love and found understanding and found hate and found humility by speaking and uttering and wiring with those *manong* phrases and words... no matter what the meanings were...Some of the corniest epitahs or words or utterances by anyone just meant that they're truer to the heart, and I believe that the spirit and sound of those words were given value...that's how it all started and all of you here are the keepers of that flame.

. . .

Erika Chong Shuch: ...I walked into this exhibit with maybe about ten television screens around the room, and on each TV screen there was the profile shot of an animal and it would show the animal standing, and a hammer would come and knock the animal on the head and the animal would die. And it looked staged to me, and it didn't look like something that was just happening in the world, like something [the artist] just happened to capture, and it didn't specify in the placards where he had gotten these images....I don't think that guy would say, "yes I'm an activist," but it activated something inside of me, and it stuck with me, and it made me think of our relationship to animals, and cruelty …I'm bringing this up because I think there's this idea that activist art is art that involves big signs and lots of puppets and lots of yelling and that this is the way to activate …but I don't believe that. The things that have been the most activating in my life were not intended to move me the way they moved me.

When I was a kid I got a microscope and I kept wanting to take it apart, and my dad kept telling me not to take it apart so I'm really the kind of person, if someone tells me to do something, I will do the opposite. So when I'm experiencing artwork that's telling me how to feel about something, it makes me shut down, I get defensive, I get pissed, I don't want to be told what to think about. I think it's such a loaded topic because we all want to create work that enriches and moves and inspires, and we are all going to be going about doing that in a different way. And I think the more diverse our vocabularies are, the better off we are to inspire action.

Carlos Villa: I agree. Good art is about questions. I try to tell my students that …I just think …no matter what you uttered would be a political act. For instance, I have a stepson whose father had passed …and somebody had looked at his dad's work in a New York gallery, and they said to him, "now what makes that art Filipino art?" and my stepson just said to him, "oh my father was Filipino." End of story.

I think that it's a new awareness. I think that at the time I came up we had to identify ourselves and we had to identify ourselves in racial terms, and we had to also say, "well Carlos Villa, he's Filipino American, Asian American, of Filipino descent, blahblahblah-blahblah," and now I don't think we have to do that. I think that my father and our fathers have fought very very hard to get to a point where all we had to do was be who we are …That's what I think …That's up to you guys to talk about what that was about!

Erika Shuch: I'm not sure of how my Asian American identity fits into my work and I think that because of my predecessors I don't have to think about it, it's just who I am. I

have yet to make work that specifically addresses those parts of my life. I've made work about my own stories but [the race/ethnic issue] hasn't come into the work yet, and I think that is a privilege.

In my opinion we're in this dire place and things are screwed up. I feel the world is just falling apart and I don't have an enormous amount of faith and hope. I want to see people act up, I want to see people be unreasonable and make crazy demands, I just want to see people make a lot of noise, and I want to see a future where young people feel inspired and impassioned to value their own stories and to value their own creativity. Because I think the problems we're facing globally are problems we're going to have to fix through creative means, we're going to have to invoke that creative spirit in order to imagine a new world. Those are my comments on the future but it's a tricky spot to be to not have hope, it's hard for me to find it.

You know when you lose hope in a relationship it makes you say "forget it, I'm just gonna be crazy because it's all gonna go down the tubes"? I just want to be crazy in my art now.

Ron Muriera: Do you feel there's a complacency among artists? Someone had asked me "do you think that API activism is dead because I don't see anything happening." So the same thing can be said within the API arts community and arts activism — has there been a comfortableness that has settled in? I think all of us on this panel are being very vocal and incorporating arts and activism in our disciplines, but do you think people have gotten very complacent in our community?

Pireeni Sundaralingam: A few years ago, if you looked to the field of literature you wouldn't see many South Asians. And now you have Pulitzer Prize winning Jhumpa Lahiri, with *The Namesake,* and VS Naipaul winning the Nobel, you see things like literary agents scouting for a South Asian writer. We joke that, as a South Asian, you just need to stand on a streetcorner with a notebook and a pen and people will throw money at you.

But then when you look more closely at the contract they're offering you, they want you to talk about your mother, or your arranged marriage. Authors: "please put your bindi on…"

I invite you to play this game: Go into a bookstore find a single book by a single South Asian contemporary artist that doesn't have a naked body, a sari, both…That's the pictorial example, it's like the door is being opened but you can only come in if you're a particular shape…The mean line running through the real demographic of South Asians in this country would probably be a Sikh cabdriver in NYC, but who's asking for his story — and it would be a man — but no one wants to hear that. So only certain types of art end up being promoted commercially.

. . .

Carlos Villa: I believe our ethos and art making are inextricable…and I'm just thinking that all of us who have who have expressive skills such as being poets — making poetry and pictures and dancing…should hook up with someone at a regular institution and come up with a team-taught curriculum that would be multidimensional and multidisciplinary. I think the time seems ripe in terms of the fact that a lot of art that's being celebrated today seems to be coming from and going away from a lot of very traditional forms, and it just seems to me that a lot of institutions would love to be able to make a connection or to value and teach those forms and make outreaches to the urban community…From my own experience it seems like the people in those institutions love to see paper that has their name on it, and all they have to do is sign off on it, and it seems like that could be a good thing…I think that those kinds of things might be a way to introduce new activism…it seems to happen in academies…I would love to see that old religion [of activism], I would love to see people with signs, I would love to see people breaking windows…and taking over!…but the thing is we participate in a more sophisticated society now, where blogs are more effective than carrying a sign…

. . .

Wei Ming Dariotis: Art is not something that sits in a museum, art is something that has the possibility of creating change in the world. Without art, we have no future. In order to be agents of change they must become artists…

. . .

Wei Ming Dariotis (to Bob Hsiang, seated in audience): Can you talk about your struggles and what you see as the new frontier for yourself as an activist artist?

Bob Hsiang: Some thirty-five years ago, Nancy Hom and I relocated from New York City. I was a pre-med student turned activist during the Vietnam War period, we demonstrated against war and we came out here pretty much during the epic battle of the I-Hotel 1974 and for three years we witnessed the transformation of I-Hotel, as ground zero for Asian Americans and other ethnicities. We saw a huge mass mobilization on Kearny Street happening against monied interests, as well as many many organizations vying for influence. It was very fascinating, a very intense microcosm of the greater struggle happening in the country. As everyone knows, the evictions took place, a hundred people or so were basically dragged out of their rooms and the hotel was demolished. The exhibit here on the right [Donna Keiko Ozawa's *Robbie Was There, I and II, see pages 28-30*] depicts one of the doors of the I-Hotel symbolically, there's the sledgehammer…

The *Activist Imagination* project — I came into it not being an artist, I don't consider myself an artist, people call me what they want. I come from a documentary point of view as a photographer witnessing the growth of movements…so I just started taking photographs and casually developed my own repertoire. I was part of the CETA program — a great program that employed a lot of unemployed artists at the time sort of inspired by the WPA project of 1930s when people were hired to do photography, mural making and all sorts of community art activity…at the time, the early '70s, we were in a deep recession, but CETA put a lot of artists to work so luckily we got some good years out of that…[*see page 18 for Bob Hsiang's work*]

Wei Ming Dariotis:…You're helping us shape reality — the way we think about it. It becomes a defiant cry, it stirs up this feeling of resistance in people. So I argue it is arts activism in both of those situations.

. . .

Stuart Gaffney (in audience): I love the interplay of art and activism. I'm so proud that my partner John and I are included among Bob's portraits for this show [*see page 24*]. And as it happened just this week the ACLU contacted us to get our picture for a story they're working on about our lawsuit for equal marriage rights for same-sex couples. Scheduling the portrait for their newsletter was proving difficult, and then we told them that actually there is this great activist portrait of us hanging at the Kearny Street Workshop gallery already — and they loved it. So now Bob's portrait of me and John will be in the ACLU newsletter next month as our case goes before California Supreme Court. So there are lots of ways large and small that activism and art connect.

I've really enjoyed this panel, in part because we've talked about the tension between art and activism, but I also want to point out that often being an artist has made me a better activist, and vice versa. We've talked about finding the front lines of activism, and it really isn't very far from here. Last week we were in the Central Valley with API Equality, standing in front of malls and asking voters not to sign the petitions being circulated to put a ban on gay marriage rights on the ballot. It was very powerful approaching people directly to talk personally about why getting married was so important to us.

It made me think, how does being an artist also make me a better activist in this instance. It was a very beautiful moment. And I thought, the tension between art and activism is good because it keeps us on our toes, but it in the end it makes us better at both.

. . .

Wei Ming Dariotis: The name "Kearny Street Workshop" doesn't say anything about those two things, it doesn't say Asian and it doesn't say art. The conversation and discussion about changing the name to something that said those two things would always come back to the local, it's a name you have to explain. And in the explaining you re-tell the stories and you reclaim that location; the name "Kearny Street Workshop" has this very specific and very local history.

Where are we? We're on Capp Street, we're nowhere near Kearny Street, but being able to reconnect with that local place - and that history - is what it's about.

. . .

Samantha Chanse (from audience): Erika, you mentioned earlier that you wanted to "go crazy" in your art-making. What does "going crazy" mean for you, and for the other panelists?

Erika Chong Shuch: Maybe it's not going crazy, it's going sane, because for me what it means personally is I'm going through this process of trying to trust myself artistically and I'm trying to trust the words that come through me and the stories that come through me and trying to not second guess myself a lot. I just came out of a year of doing work about the effects of incarceration on people who are left on the outside, it's a territory where there are so many rights and wrongs. I don't want to think about what's right and wrong, what is right and wrong politically, I just want to trust that what I feel passionate about will resonate…A fierce loyal trust of instinct.

Ron Muriera: Going crazy for me is reminding myself of the joy of being an activist-artist artist-activist. I do that by pulling out my accordion. The accordion holds a deep connection for me because I was part of a group in San Francisco called Those Darn Accordions and we were known for doing *accordionista* raids in restaurants throughout San Francisco where fifty accordions would bust into a restaurant playing "Lady of Spain." Our goal was to bring respect back to the accordion. I like to think of ourselves as squeeze box activists.

Carlos Villa: Every time I get involved in a project, my wife tells me I'm going crazy. It's always been the way it happens, it's a constant…so I don't know…basically I think that you not only have to speak your mind, but-you have to act your mind and I think that those actions go beyond "art," it goes beyond community I guess. You have to admit that those actions for the community start with admitting that what you are doing starts from being "selfish" — that you would do "whatever" — without expecting a reward or commendation…you do it because of *Utang* [soulful pinoy payback honoring your forebearers]…that having spoken with folks in the community about something that you have all been thinking about, and feeling resonance…But the thing is you just have to do what you think you need to do…I guess maybe that's going crazy.

ONGOING, NOVEMBER 2007 – PRESENT
Activist Imagination **Blog. On-line conversation.**

FROM A DECEMBER 30, 2007 POST ENTITLED "WHY I AM NOT MAKING ACTIVIST ART FOR ACTIVIST IMAGINATION," BY CHRISTINE WONG YAP:

In the context of a show called Activist Imagination, I have to assume part of the show's audience expects Activist art. For the best viewing experiences, though, I hope viewers approach Activist art and contemporary art with their respective criteria in mind.

I believe Activist art, above all, values function. It privileges political soundness — what is the message and is it on point? Do you agree or not? Visually, Activist Art tends to embrace beauty, decoration, style, visual incident. Like advertisements, engagement is primarily through the eyes and the heart (the most effective pieces usually convey passion, outrage, empathy, guilt, etc.).

Contemporary art, on the other hand, engages form, as well as the careful consideration of conceptual or art-historical soundness. True to stereotype, this does require some education. But it also requires receptivity to appreciate contemporary arts' expanded areas of experimentation: assumptions about beauty, value and art itself are up for grabs for artists' use. Engaging contemporary art is at least as much intellectual as it is visual.

While Activist art challenges political beliefs, contemporary can be a more challenging art experience. I can't see why those who wish to disrupt the status quo would not appreciate both kinds of challenges.

An exhibition of reproductions
of Kearny Street Workshop posters
curated by Christopher Wong Doyle

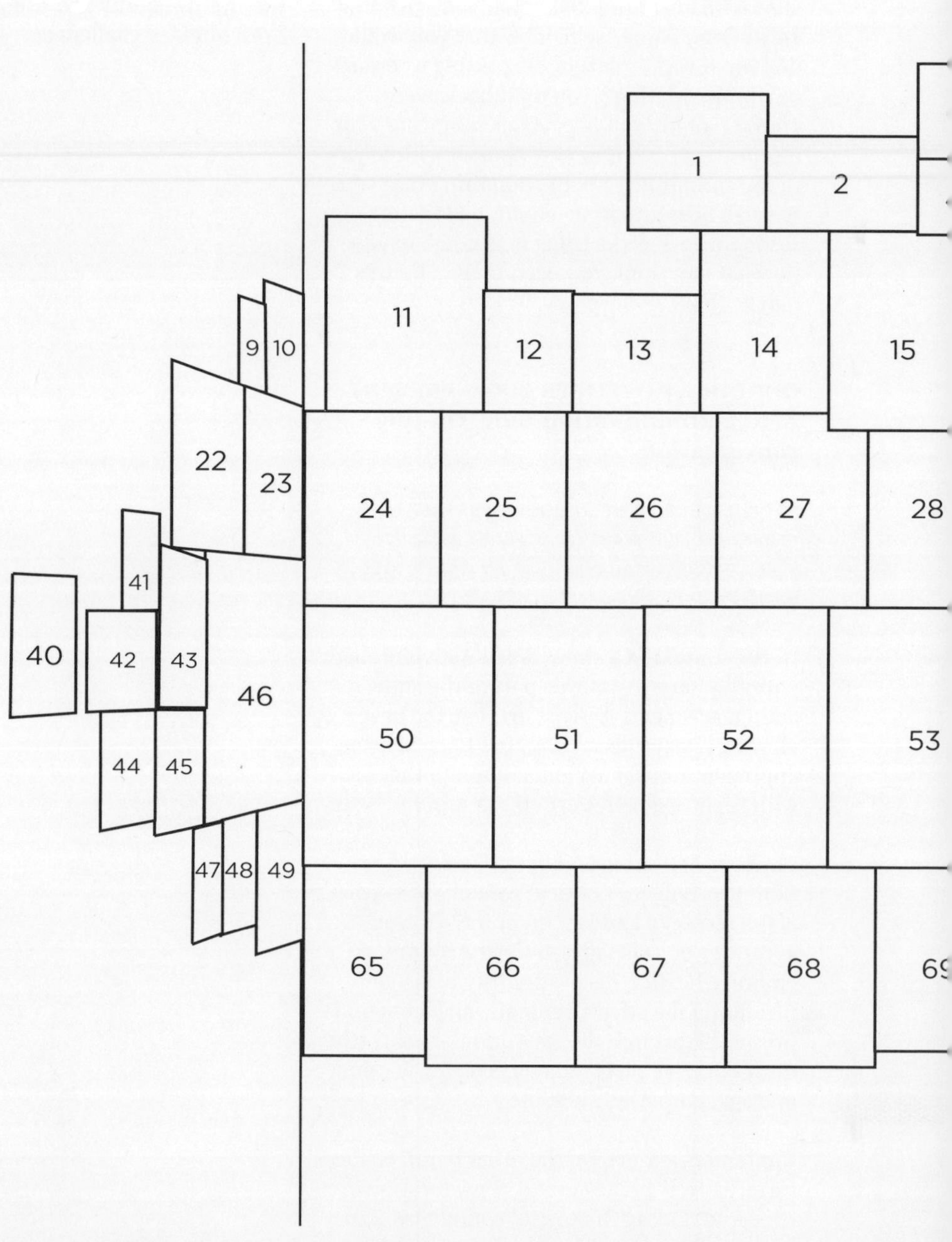

57 KSW POSTERS

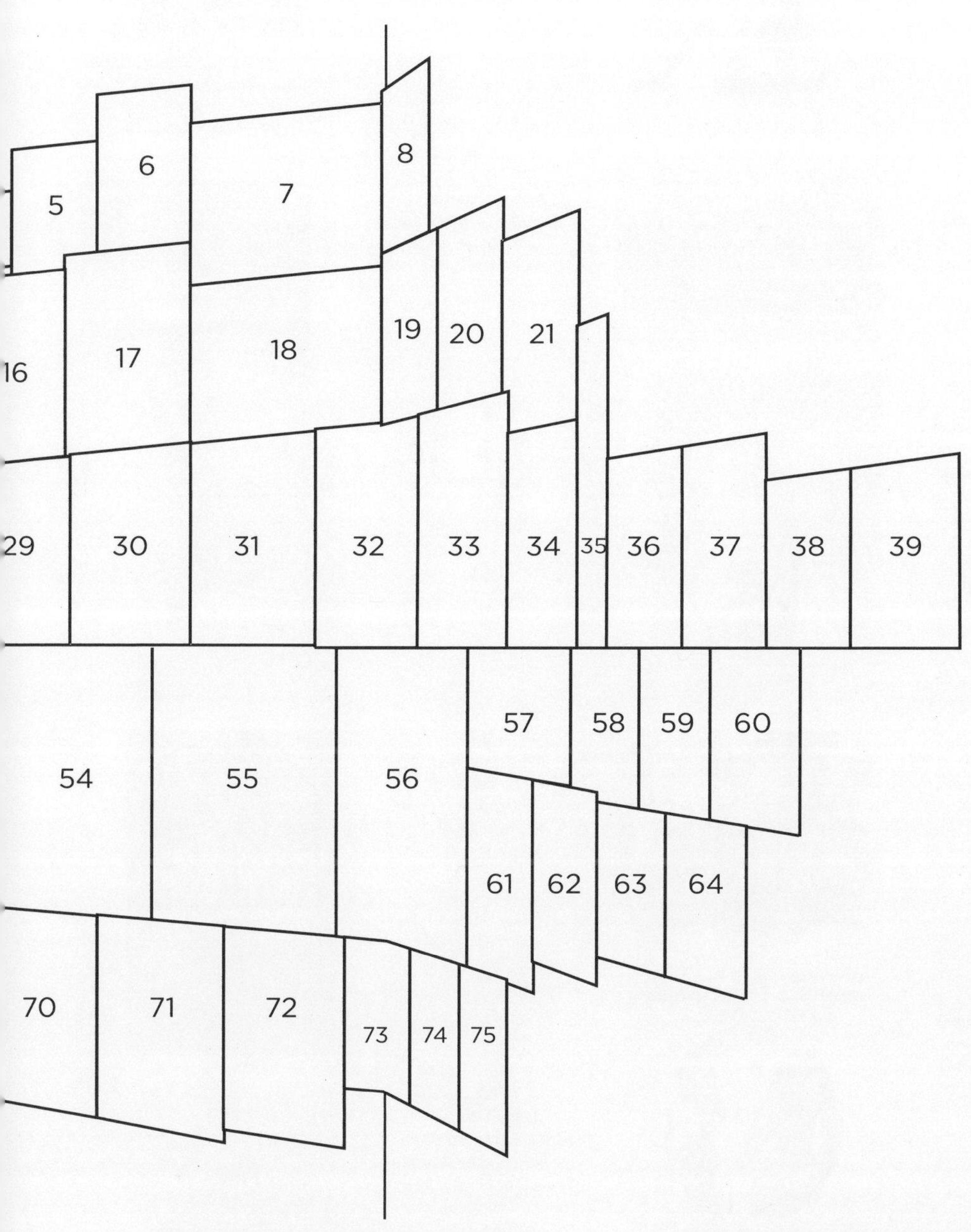

All images remain copyright of the original artists.

The images in this exhibit are digital reproductions photographed by Yap at the California Ethnic and Multicultural Archives (CEMA) at the Davidson Library at UC Santa Barbara in October 2007.

Special thanks to CEMA Director Sal Guerena, Sam Chanse, Zand Gee, Nancy Hom and Leland Wong.

1
Artist unknown
Title unknown
n.d.
14 in. x 15 in.

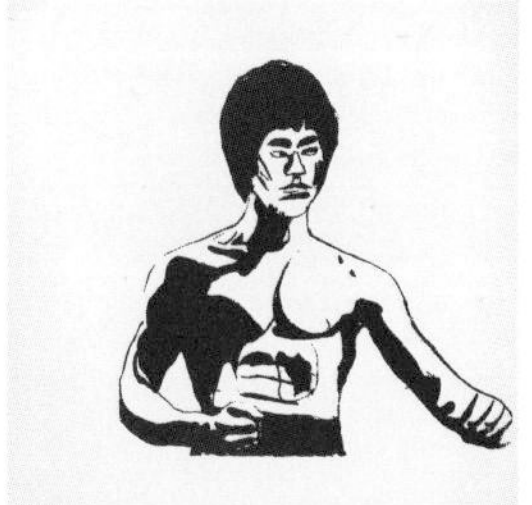

2
Artist unknown
KSW's 10th anniversary
1982
17 in. x 11 in.

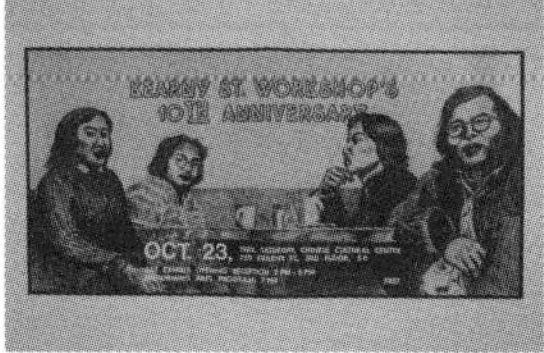

3
Leland Wong
*An art exhibit and open house
by members of
Kearny Street Workshop*
n.d.
8.5 in. x 14 in.

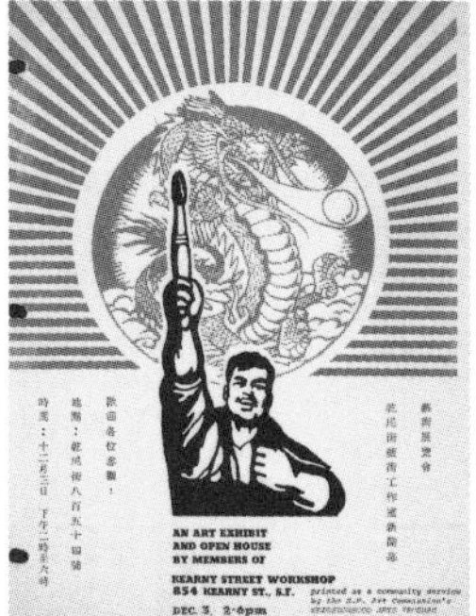

4
Artist unknown
*Rene Mederos: Cuban Silk-
screens of Vietnam.*
n.d.
11 in. x 17 in.

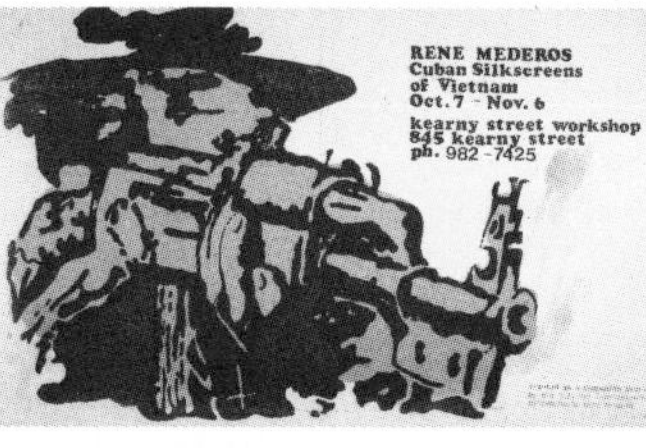

5
Leland Wong
*Asian American Summer
Art Workshops in ceramics,
photography, silkscreen*
n.d.
10 in. x 13 in.

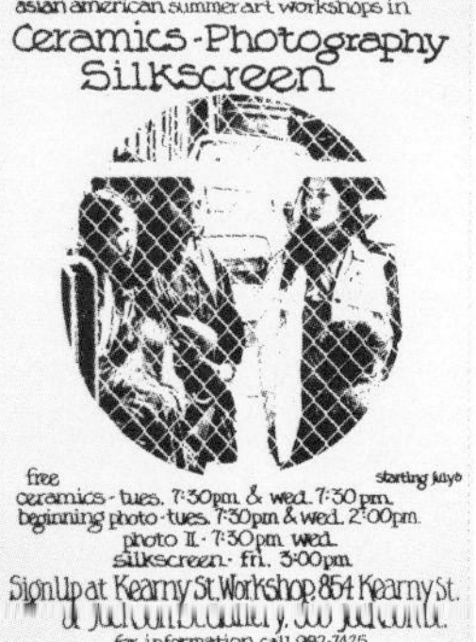

6
Nancy Hom
*Unbound Feet Presents
Yellow Daughters*
1980
14 in. x 17 in.

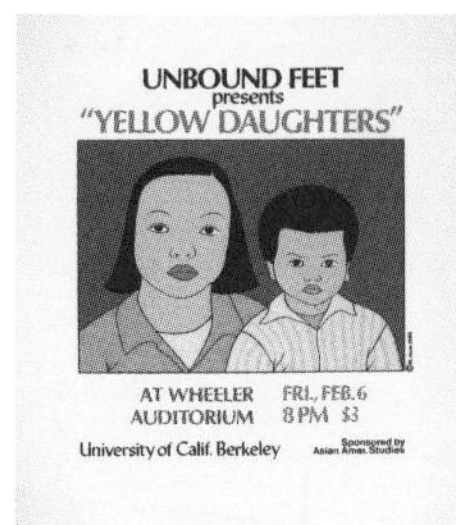

7
Artist unknown
Oshogatsu 1979 Festival
1979
23 in. x 17.5 in.

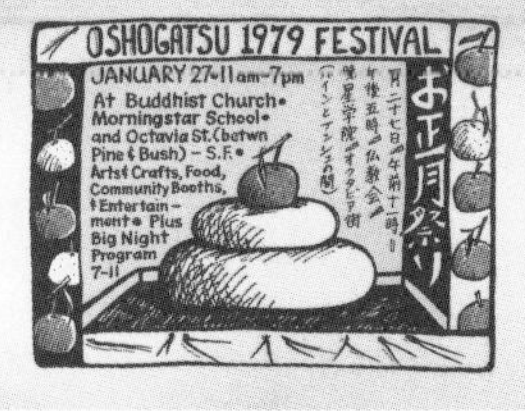

8
Artist unknown
*Boycott Kinetsu: We Shall
Not Be Moved*
n.d.
10 in. x 14.25 in.

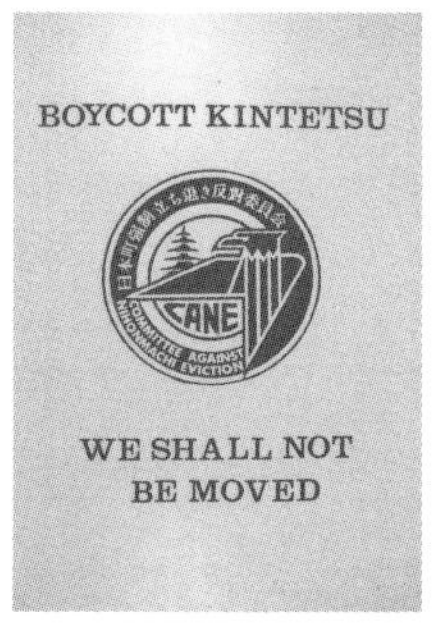

9
Artist unknown
Jingle Bell Rock
1980
8.5 in. x 5.5 in.

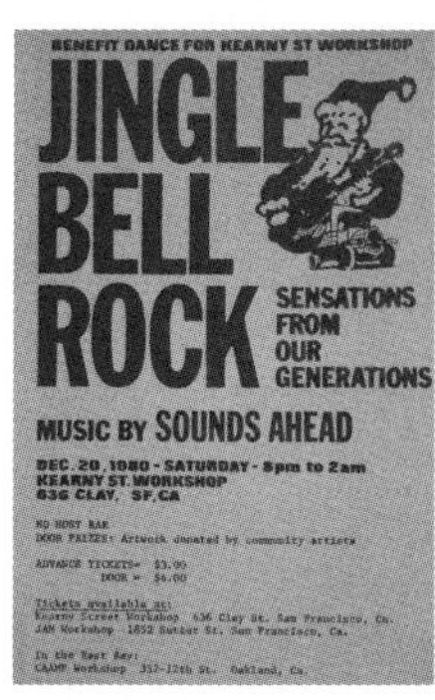

10
Leland Wong
*Jackson Street Gallery
presents… The World
Travels of Freddy Mar*
1975
8.5 in. x 11 in.

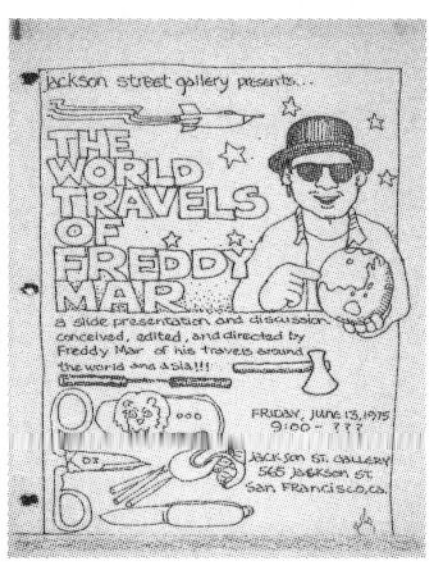

11
Artist unknown
(© International Hotel
Tenants Association)
*Supermanong! Peace
with a Lease*
1975
17 in. x 22 in.

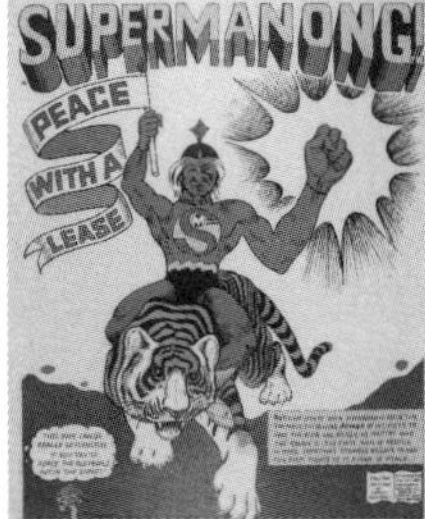

16
Leland Wong
Arts and Crafts Workshops
n.d.
13 in. x 20 in.

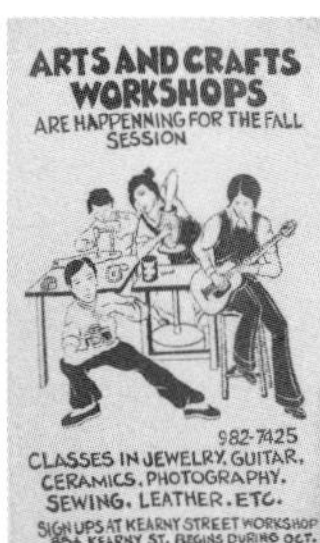

12
Artist unknown
*Neighbor exhibition
announcement*
n.d.
8.5 in. x 14 in.

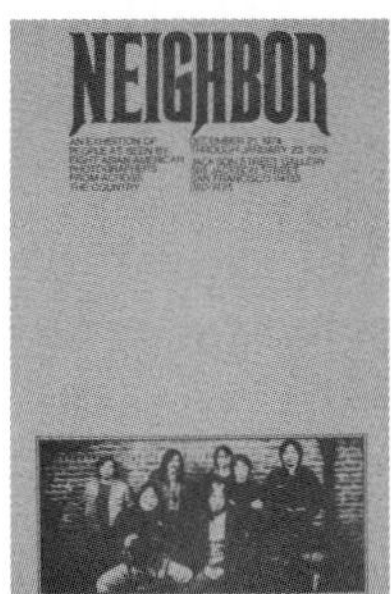

17
Artist unknown
*Isuda Ti Immuna,"they who
were first"*
1976
15.5 in. x 20 in.

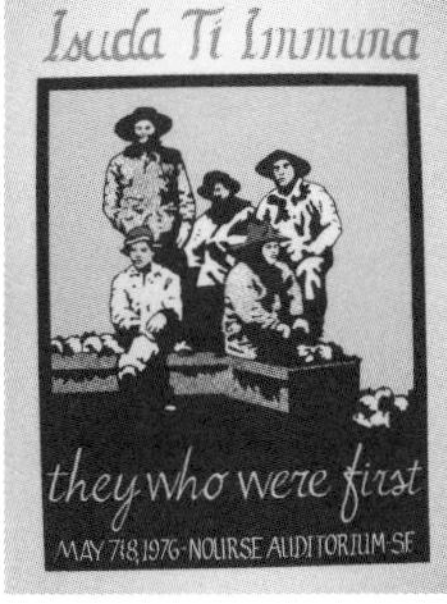

13
Nancy Hom
Poetry & Music
1978
13.75 in. x 13 in.

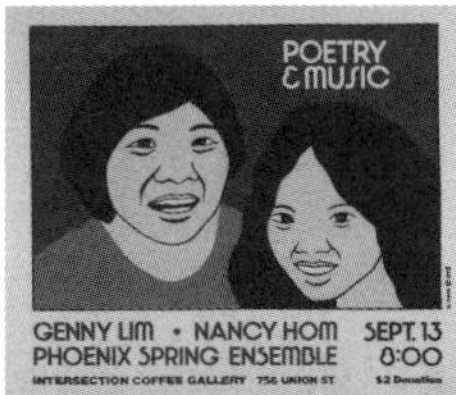

18
Artist unknown
Chinese Spring Festival
1977
23 in. x 17.5 in.

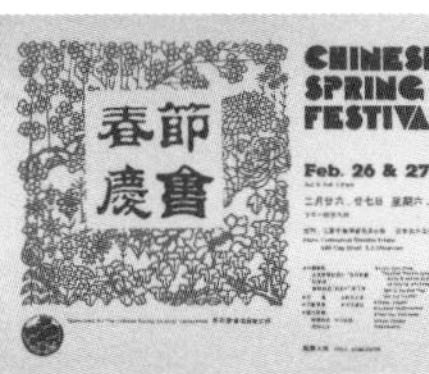

14
Leland Wong
*World travels of Freddy Mar
Part 2*
1977
14 in. x 20.5 in.

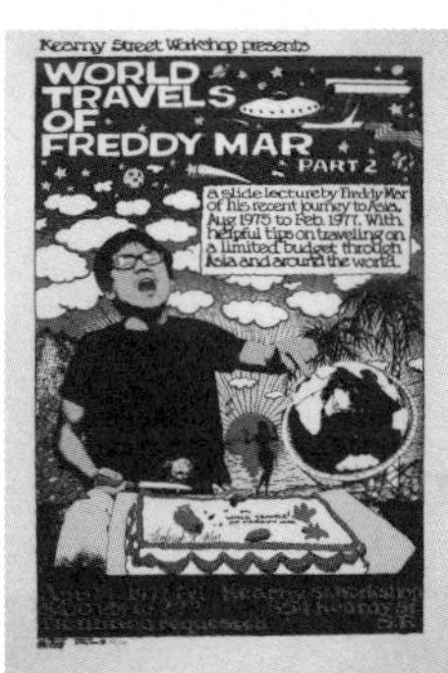

19
Jack Loo
*Juramentado,
Bayani Mariano*
n.d.
12 in. x 18 in.

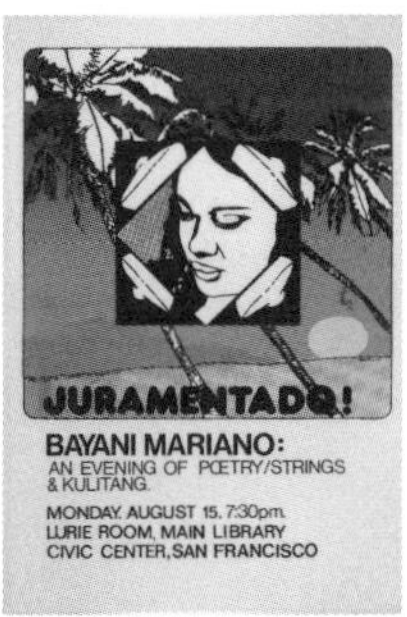

15
Jack Loo
*Asian American poetry
reading*
1976
14 in. x 17.5 in.

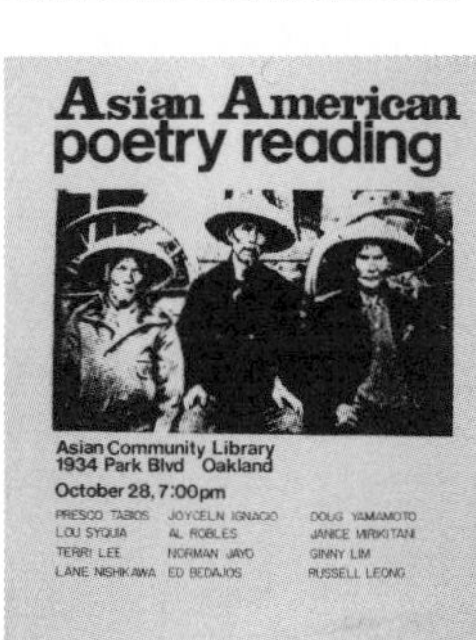

20
Artist unknown
*J.T. Funk & Soul Benefit Dance
for Vietnamese Orpanages*
1973
12 in. x 18.25 in.

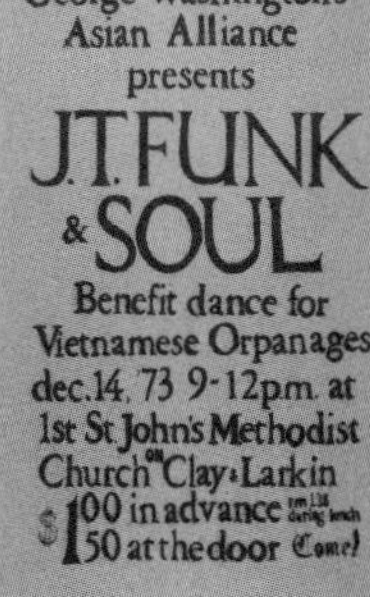

21
Artist unknown
Wilma Pang Sings Chinese Songs with the Chinese Instrumental Ensemble
n.d.
12.5 in. x 18 in.

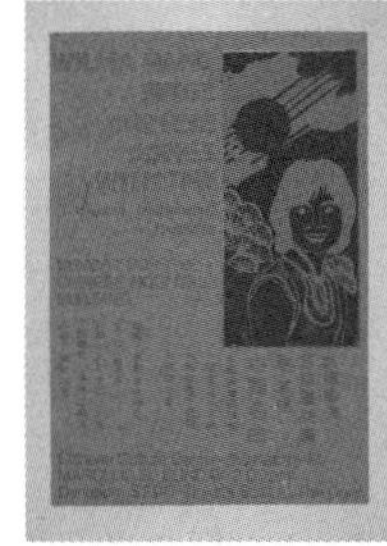

22
Jack Loo
6th Annual Hop Jok Fair
1979
13 in. x 16.5 in.

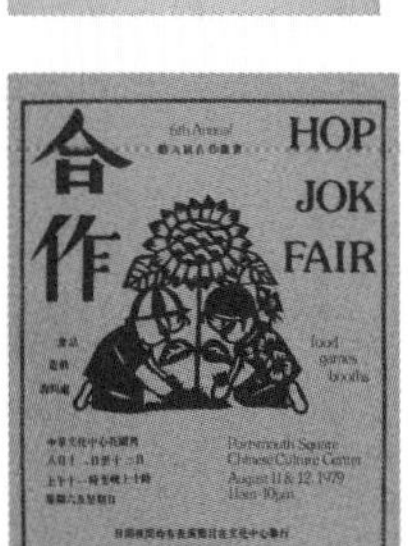

23
Zand Gee
Asian American Jazz Festival
1983
17.5 in. x 23 in.

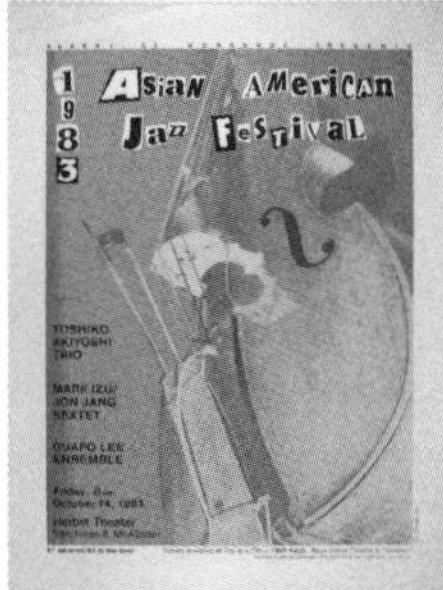

24
Artist unknown
Third World Photography
n.d.
13 in. x 20 in.

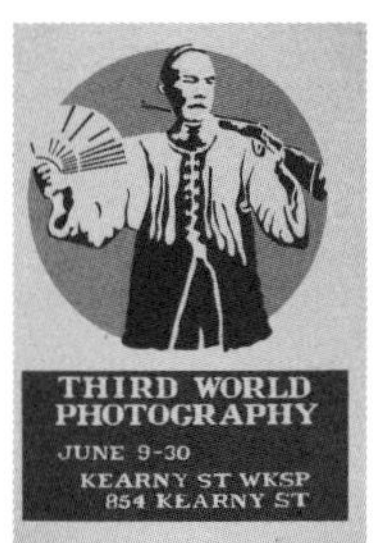

25
Leland Wong
Angel Island, an exhibition of the Chinese experience at the immigration station
1976
14.5 in. x 21 in.

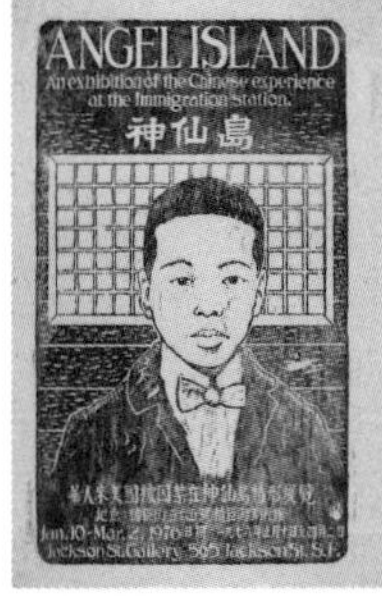

26
Artist unknown
Keep District Elections! No on A & B
n.d.
17.5 in. x 23 in.

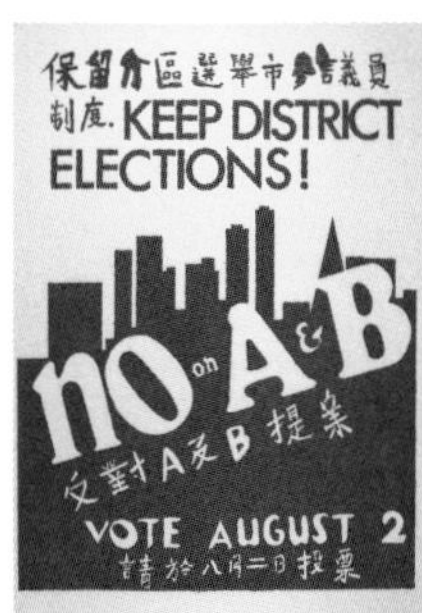

27
Artist unknown
Celebrate the May 4th Movement
1975
17.5 in. x 23 in.

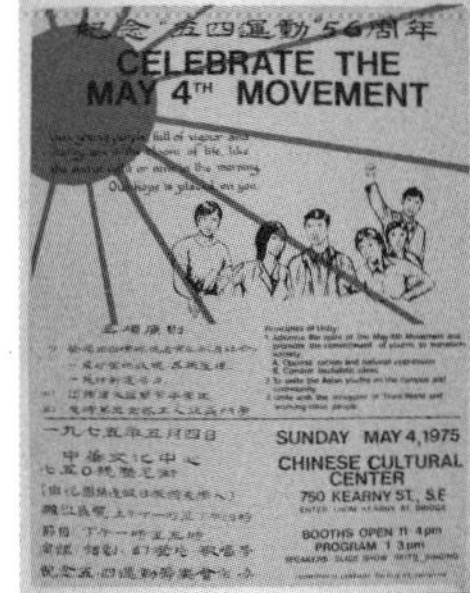

28
Leland Wong
Jackson Street Gallery Grand Opening
1974
13 in. x 20 in.

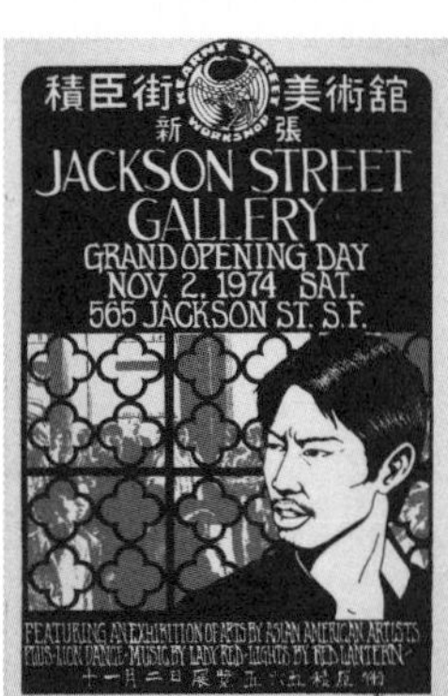

29
Artist unknown
June 16th Community Fair
n.d.
13 in. x 20 in.

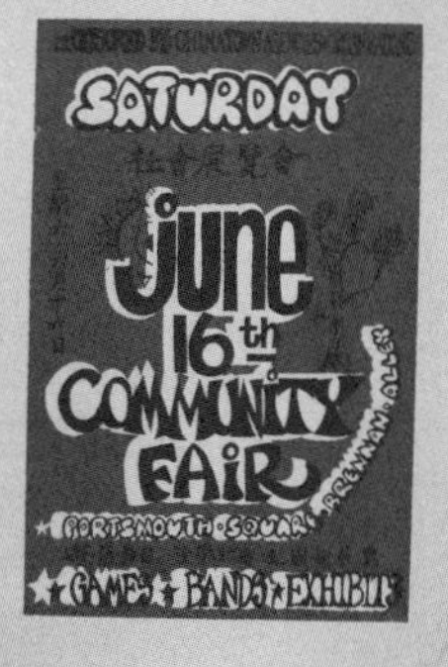

30
Artist unknown
*Konko Church Benefit Bazaar,
Summer Festival*
n.d
14 in. x 20.5 in.

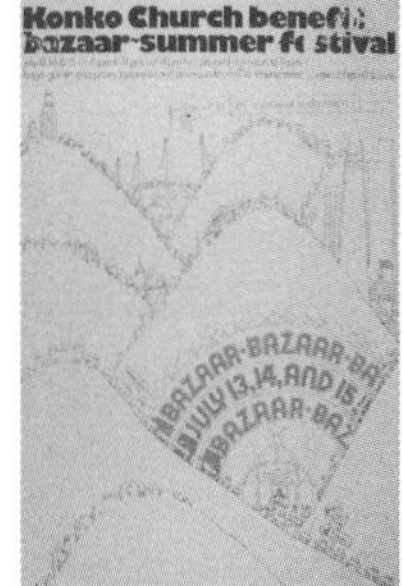

31
Artist unknown
*Summer Happenings, China-
town-Northbeach Area Youth
Council and Kearny Street
Workshop Co-sponsors*
n.d.
13 in. x 20 in.

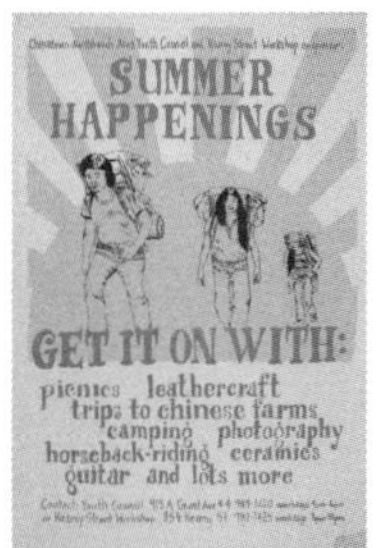

32
Artist unknown
Pamana , '75 (Heritage)
n.d.
14 in. x 22 in.

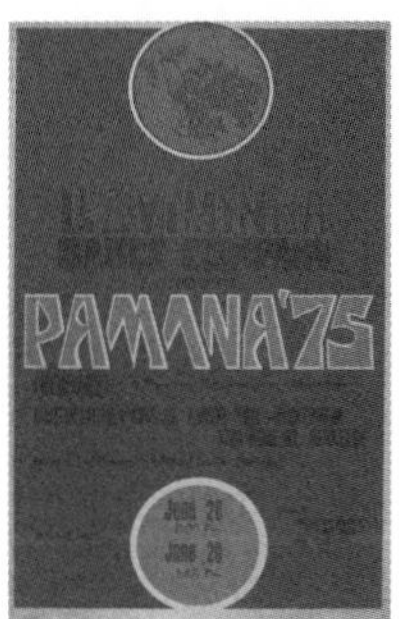

33
Artist unknown
Ap-Apong-a-Baak
n.d.
17 in. x 23 in.

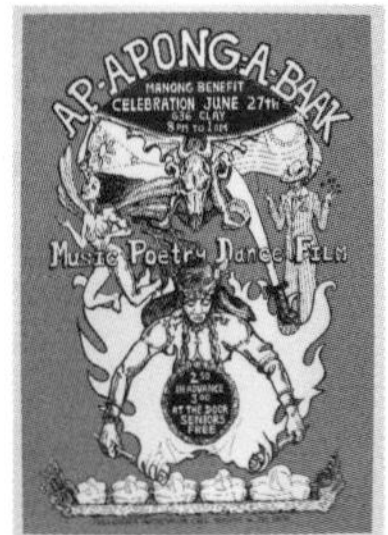

34
Zand Gee
Woman from Hiroshima
1980
11.5 in. x 17.5 in.

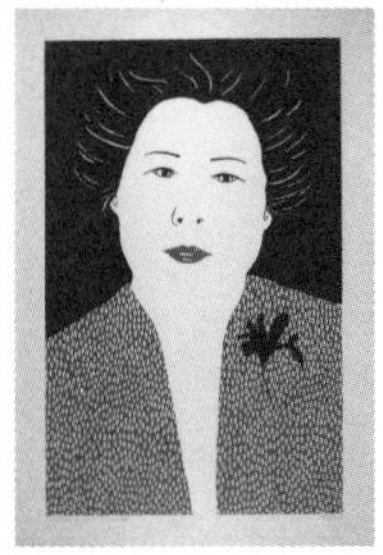

35
Leland Wong
*Asian Community Silkscreen
Graphics Workshop*
n.d.
4 in. x 24 in.

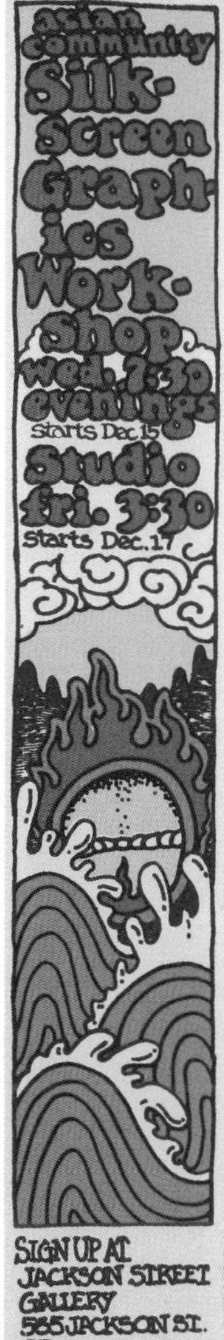

36
Artist unknown
*Master Chinese Ballet &
Folkloric Dance Workshop*
n.d.
8.5 in. x 14 in.

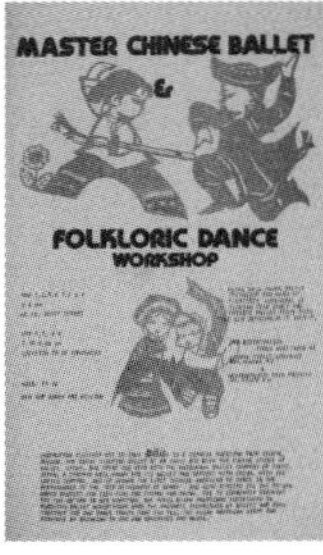

37
Designer unknown
Juan Fuentes and Rupert Garcia: July 5 – Aug 16, Jackson St Gallery.
n.d.
8.5 in. x 14 in.

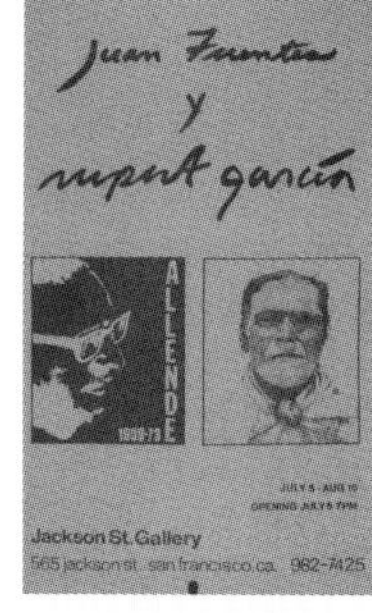

38
Nancy Hom
Bob Hsiang Photography Class flyer
1982
8.5 in. x 11 in.

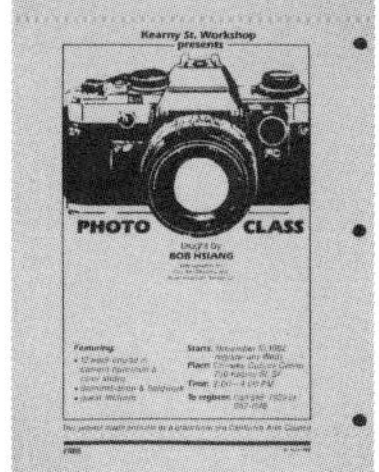

39
Nancy Hom
Bob Hsiang Photography Class flyer
1982
8.5 in. x 11 in.

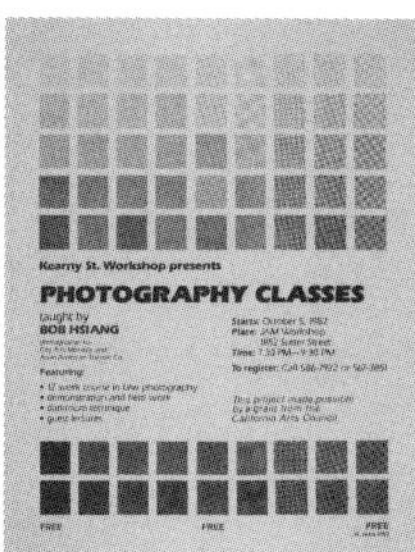

40
Author unknown
Declaration and Aims & Goals.
n.d.
8.5 in. x 11 in.

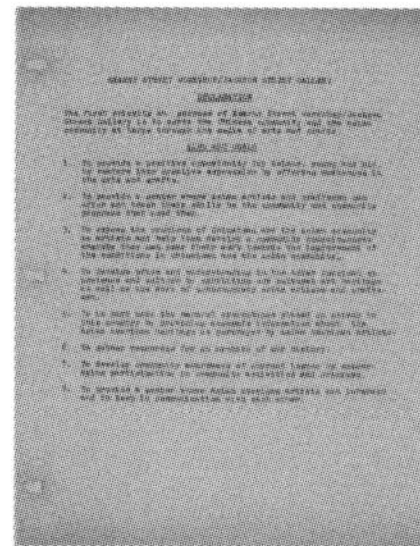

41
Artist unknown
KSW 10th anniversary program
1982
8.5 in. x 11 in. flat
5.5 in. x 8.5 in. folded

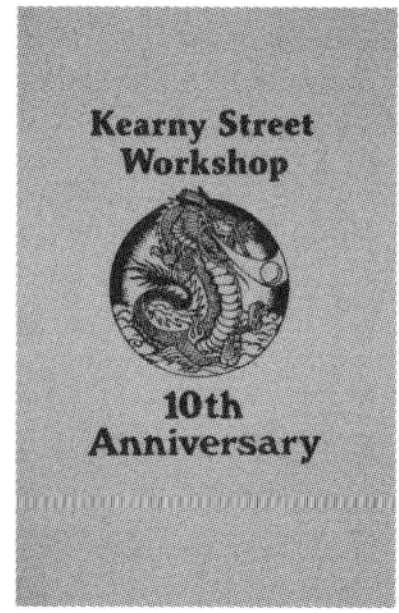

42
Author unknown
Mission Statement: Who We Are
n.d.
8.5 in. x 11 in.

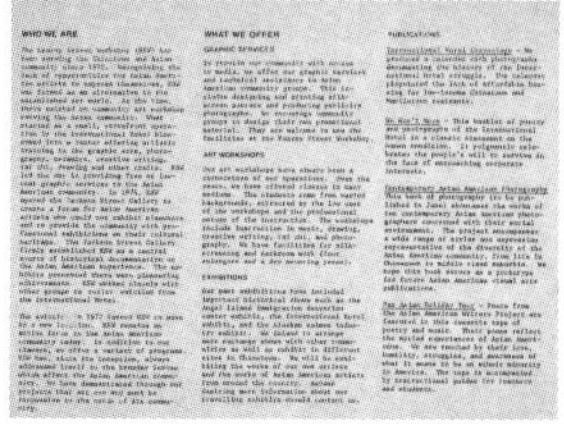

43
Author unknown
"The I-Hotel Still Stands!" Newsleaflet of the International Hotel Tenants Association
January 7, 1978
dimensions unavailable

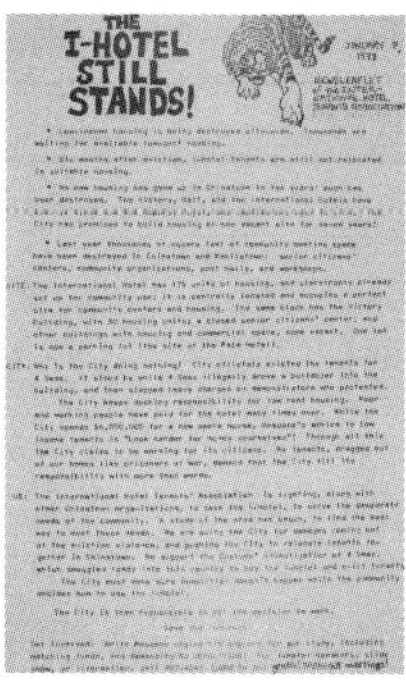

44
Author unknown
Kearny Street Workshop brochure
n.d.
7 in. x 8.5 in. folded
21 in. x 8.5 in. flat

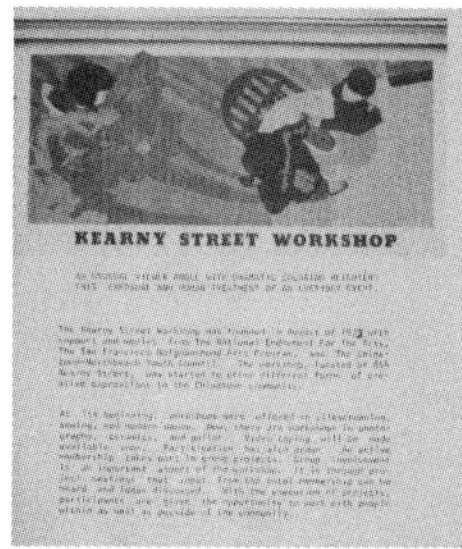

45
Leland Wong
KSW logo leaflet on classes
n.d.
8.5 in. x 11 in.

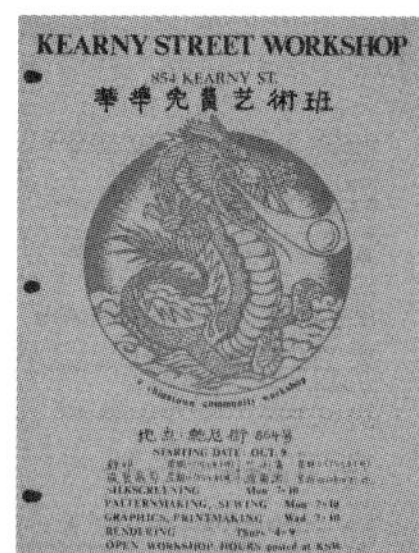

46
Artist unknown
Take Up the Struggle / Demand Our Full Rights
n.d.
19 in. x 25 in.

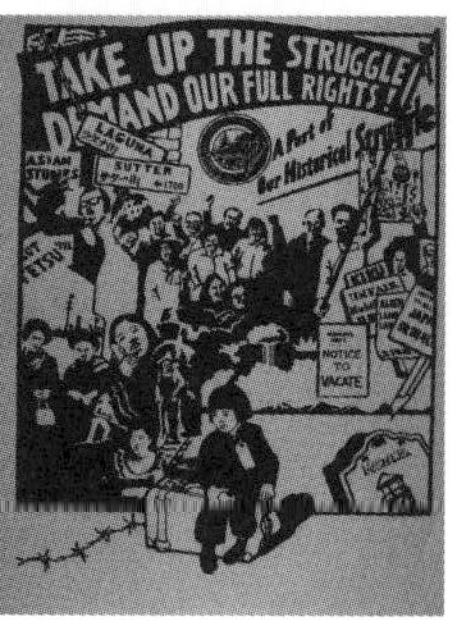

47
Artist unknown
*Angel Island exhibition
announcement*
n.d.
4.25 in. x 8.5 in.

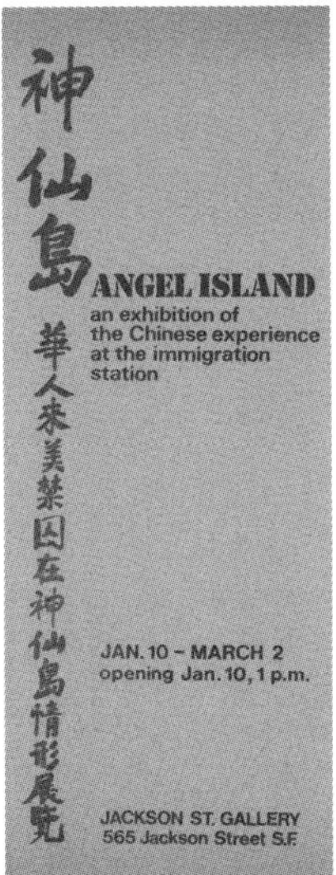

48
Artist unknown
*Gold Mountain on the
silver screen*
1975
8.5 in. x 11 in.

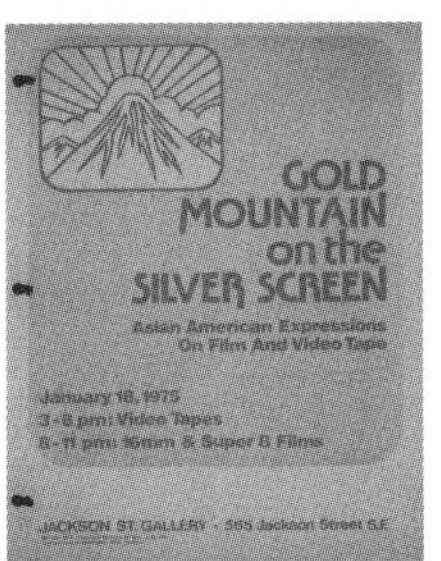

49
Artist unknown
*International Hotel
Cultural Series*
n.d.
8.5 in. x 14 in.

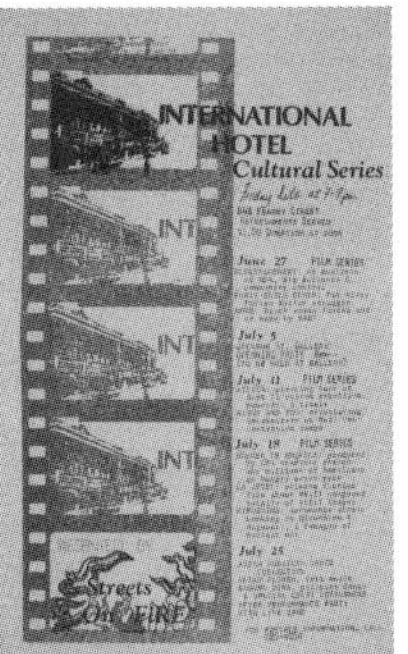

50
Leland Wong
*Asian American Media
Communications
Presents: Coming
Together*
1973
20 in. x 26 in.

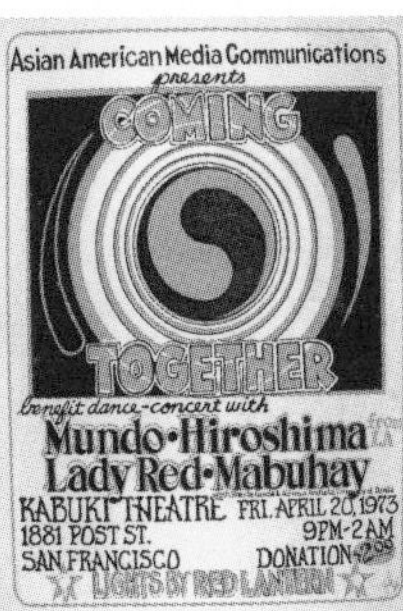

51
Artist unknown
Save International Hotel
n.d.
15.25 in. x 26 in.

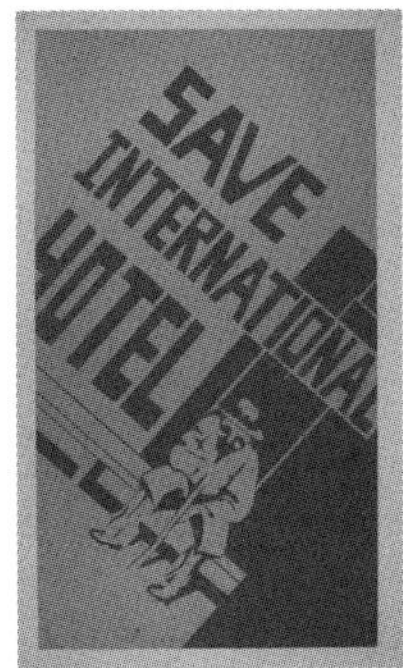

52
Artist unknown
*A Benefit for the Kearny Street
Workshop Programs. Presents
"Feelin' Good"*
n.d
20 in. x 26 in.

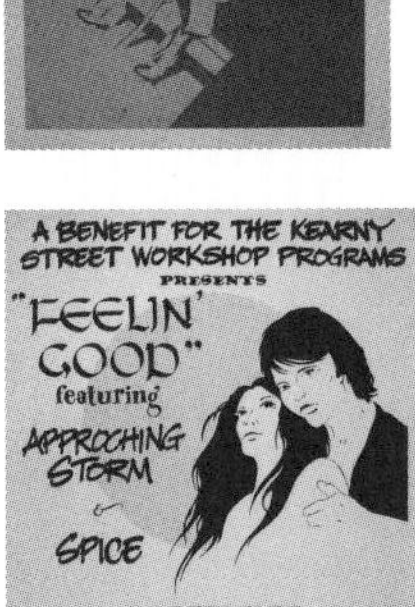

53
Artist unknown
*Bay Area Overseas
Chinese Students Drama Club:
Thunder Storm*
n.d.
20 in. x 26 in.

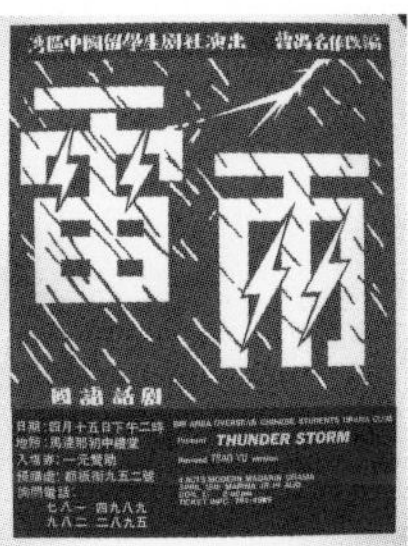

54
Artist unknown
*Friendship. Panda bear and
Snoopy holding hands.*
n.d.
20 in. x 26 in.

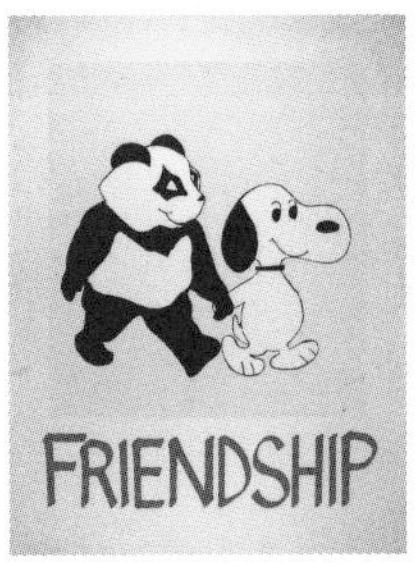

55
Mitsui Murai
Oshogatsu Festival
1977
20 in. x 26 in.

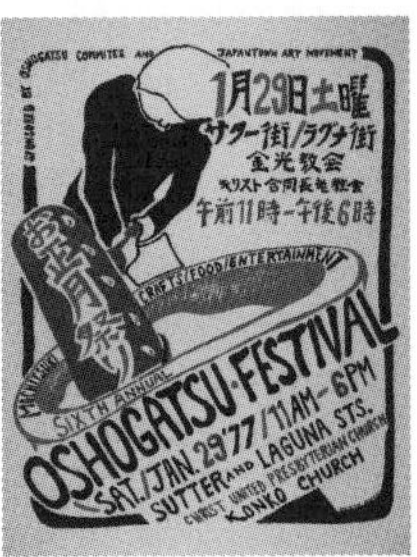

56
Artist unknown
*A Benefit for the Chinatown
Summer Youth Program,
Natural High*
n.d.
20 in. x 26 in.

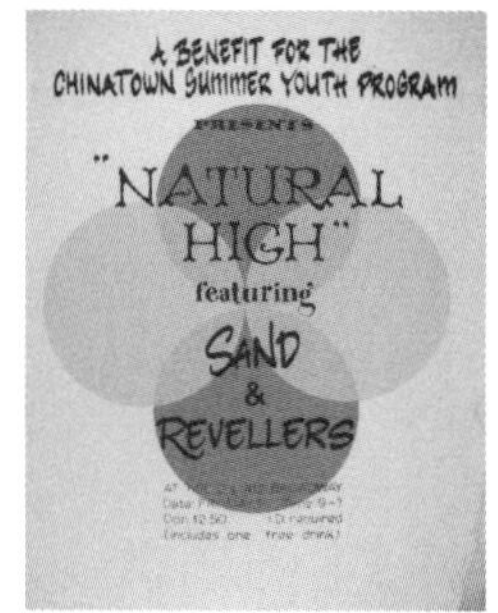

57
Zand Gee
*Oldies but Goodies, dance
music of the 50's & 60's*
1979
20 in. x 13 in.

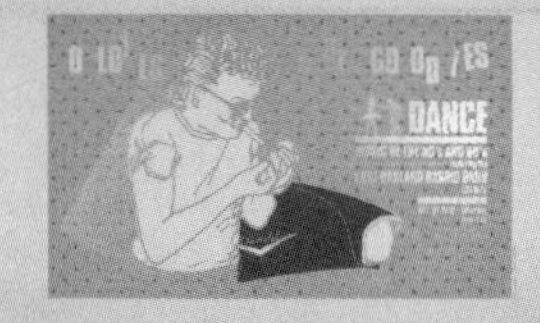

58
Photo by Chris Huie /
Designer unknown
*Fall of the I-Hotel screening
flyer*
1984
8.5 in. x 11 in.

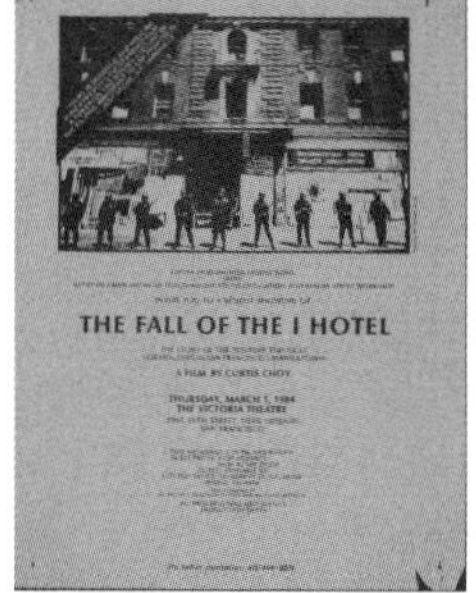

59
Artist unknown
*Beware! Dec 7. Asian Jazz &
Blues Poetry*
n.d.
8.5 in. x 11 in.

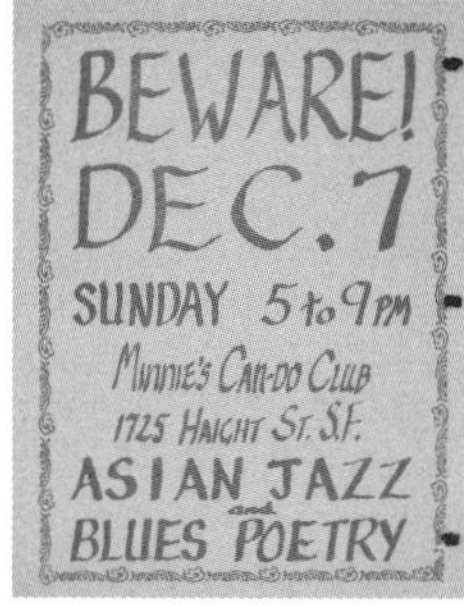

60
Leland Wong
*Jackson St Gallery red and
black poster*
1974
8.5 in. x 11 in.

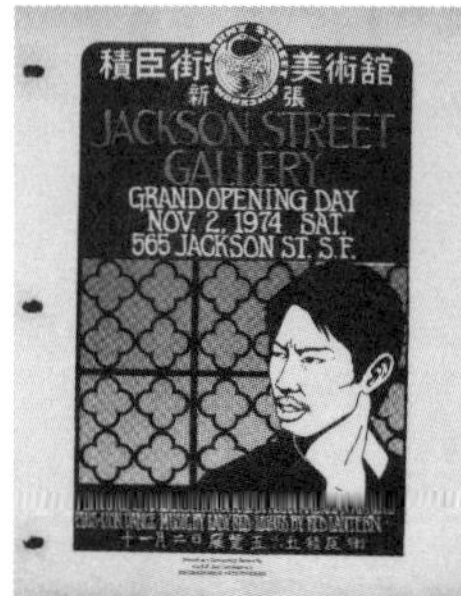

61
Artist unknown
*Mga Kababayan
International Hotel*
n.d.
11 in. x 17 in.

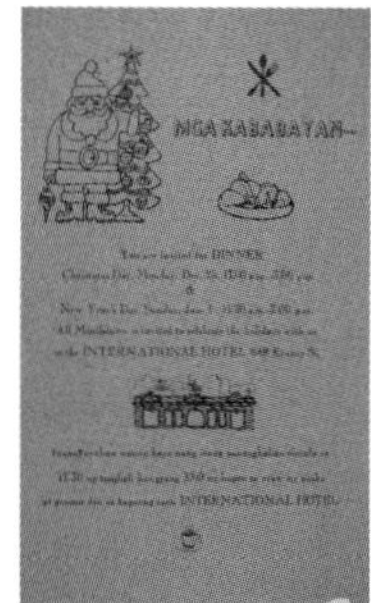

62
Artist unknown
*A photographic history
of Asian Americans
in the northwest salmon
industry*
1977
8.5 in. x 14 in.

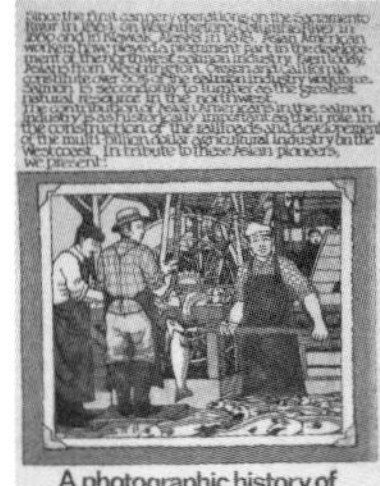

63
Artist unknown
*Celebration! Manilatown
Senior Center*
n.d.
8.5 in. x 11 in.

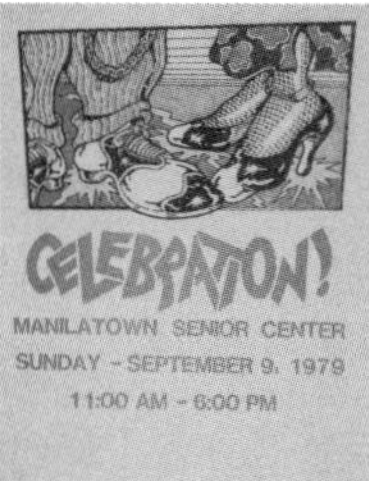

64
Zand Gee
*Asian American Jazz Fest
program cover*
1982
8.5 in. x 11 in.

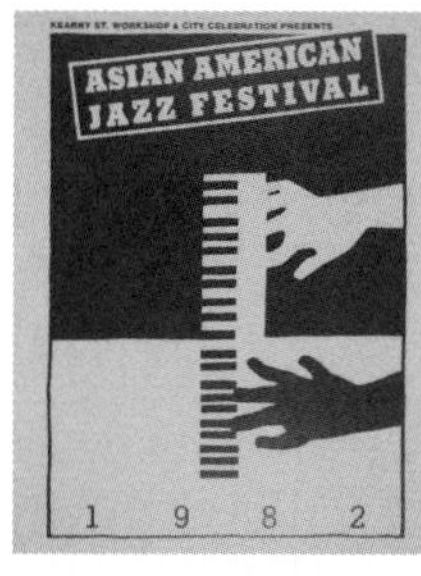

65
Leland Wong
*Chinatown North Beach Area
Youth Council's Toy Drive*
n.d.
13 in. x 20 in.

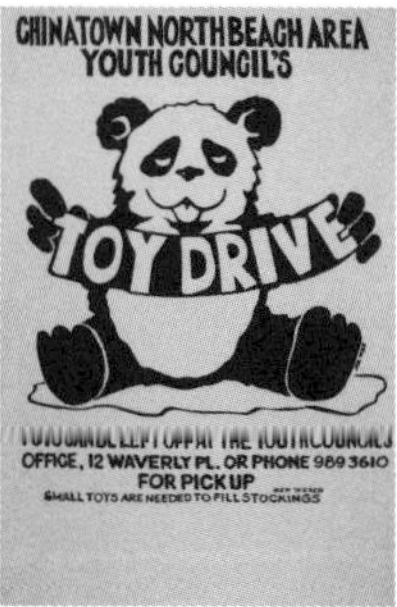

65 KSW POSTERS

66
Jack Loo
2nd Annual Pilipino Lechon Celebration
1978
17.5 in. x 24 in.

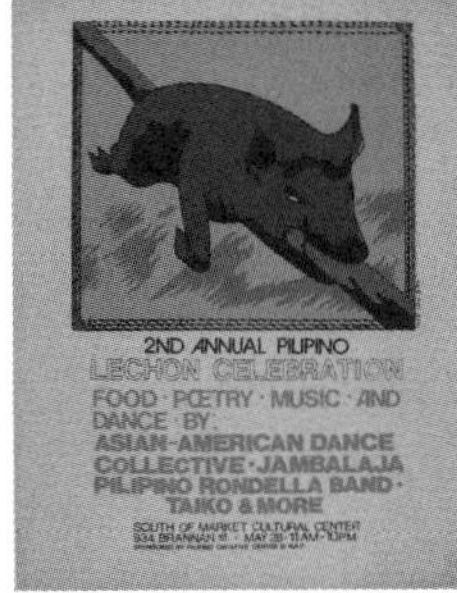

67
Artist unknown
Committee for True Representation of China
1974
17 in. x 22.5 in.

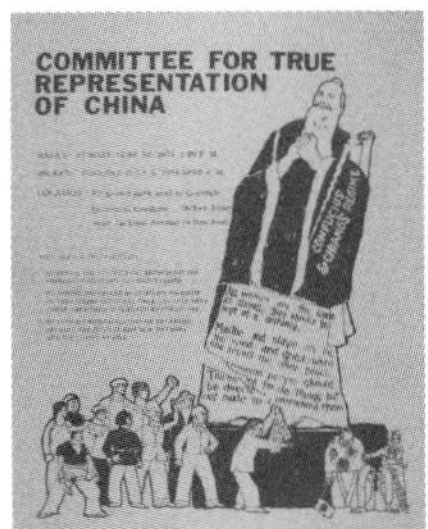

68
Artist unknown
Nihonmachi Gardens Opening
n.d.
17.5 in. x 23 in.

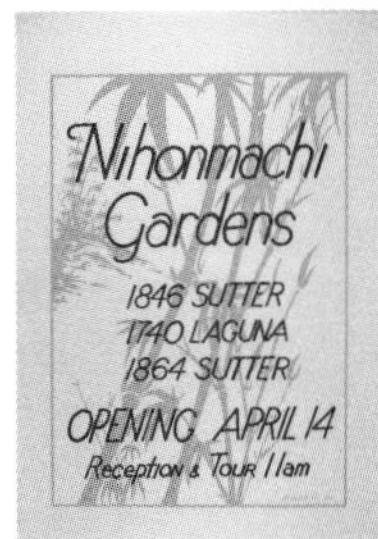

69
Artist unknown
Chinese Spring Festival
1975
13 in. x 20 in.

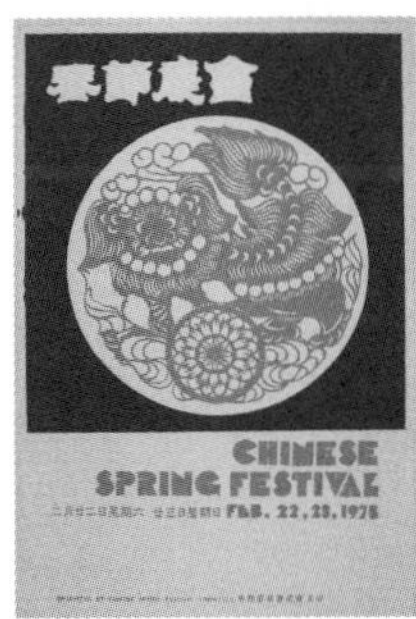

70
Leland Wong
1st Annual Nihonmachi Street Fair
1974
17.5 in. x 23 in.

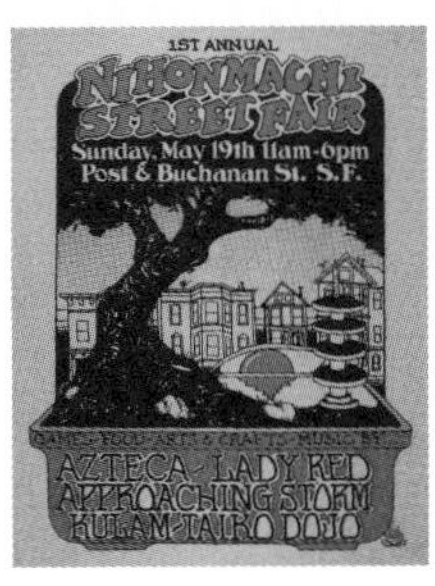

71
Artist unknown
Title unknown
n.d.
14 in. x 22 in.

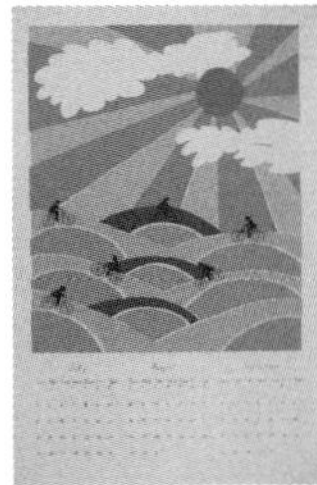

72
Artist unknown
Youth Service Center, Richmond Office
n.d.
13 in. x 20 in.

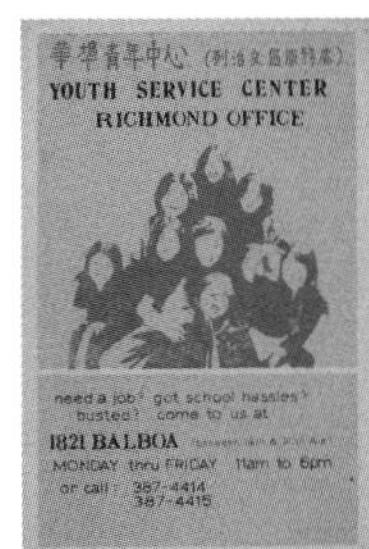

73
Artist unknown
Members of the Asian-American Writers Workshop will be reading from their works at East Wind Bookstore
n.d.
8.5 in. x 14 in.

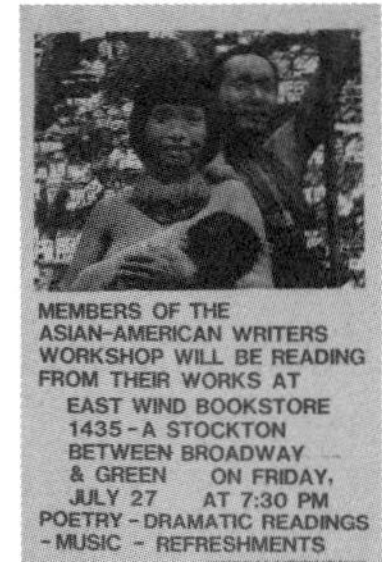

74
Artist unknown
Isuda Ti Immuna play broadside
n.d.
8.5 in. x 14 in.

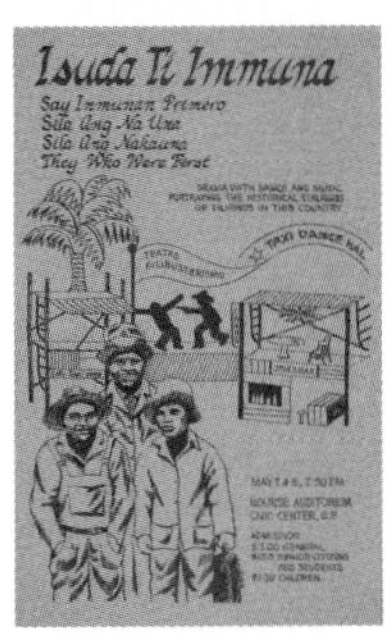

75
Artist unknown
Poetry Music Films Fridays International Hotel
n.d.
8.5 in. x 14 in.

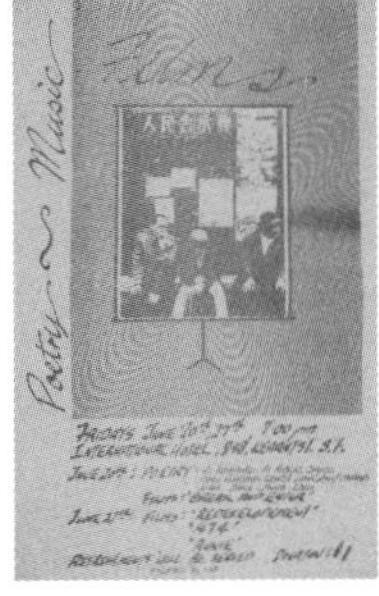

BOB HSIANG

Bob Hsiang was born in New York City in 1948. After attending Stuyvesant High School, he enrolled at State University of New York at Buffalo as a biology major. It was in Buffalo where he became interested in photography. He became photo editor of the university newspaper where he covered various events on and off campus, while also taking several art courses that included photographic aesthetics. After finishing school around 1971, he became involved in the emerging Asian American movement and, while living near Chinatown, he began to document the neighborhood and various Asian American anti-war activities in New York City. He helped start the Asian Media Collective, a group of community activists who used multimedia to advocate against the Vietnam War and build Asian American consciousness.

After moving to San Francisco, he joined with Kearny Street Workshop in documenting the activities at the International Hotel in 1974. Professionally, he taught photo classes at the de Young Museum Art School and worked as a museum photographer. During the 1980s, he began a freelance business using his skills as a photojournalist and object photographer. Concurrently, he was the resident photographer for the Asian American Theater Company and also worked with the Asian American Jazz Festival.

Presently, he divides his professional activities between corporate and non-profit organizations, specializing in annual reports, brochures and marketing for the web and in print. He is also serving as an advisor to Kearny Street Workshop and a contractor for Manilatown Cultural Foundation and the Chinese Culture Center.
www.bobhsiangphoto.com

Selected Exhibitions:

2008
Activist Imagination, Kearny Street Workshop, San Francisco, CA.

2006
MacArthur Street Corridor Portraits, Mills College, Oakland, CA.

2005
Unsung Opera, San Francisco Public Library, San Francisco, CA.

2002
The AAAC Story, Asian American Arts Centre, New York, NY.

2001
The Whole World is Watching, Berkeley Art Center, Berkeley, CA.

Other Exhibitions/Venues:

2000
3 Decades of Kearny Street Workshop Artists, Chinese Historical Society of America, San Francisco, CA.

1998
Celebrating the Arts, ODC Theater Gallery, San Francisco, CA.

1997
Kearny Street Workshop 10th Anniversary Exhibition, TODCO Woolf House, San Francisco, CA.

1996
Asian American Jazz Makers, Chinatown Community Arts Gallery, San Francisco, CA.

1992
Pursuing Wild Bamboo: Portraits of Asian American Artists, Ohana Cultural Center, Oakland, CA.

1991
Pursuing Wild Bamboo: Portraits of Asian American Artists, Chinatown Community Arts Gallery, San Francisco, CA.

1990
Bay Area Artists, Performing Arts Library and Museum Permanent Collection, San Francisco, CA.

1989
Kearny Street Workshop Photographers, Chinatown Community Arts Gallery, San Francisco, CA.

1985
Dejá Vu: Photos of the Asian American Theater Company, People's Theater Coalition, San Francisco, CA.

1982
Kearny Street Workshop 10th Anniversary Exhibition, Chinatown Community Arts Gallery, San Francisco, CA.

1981
Photo Exhibition, Manilatown Senior Center, San Francisco, CA.

1976
Angel Island, Jackson Street Gallery, San Francisco, CA.

1975
PINOTOH (People in Need of Their Own Housing), Jackson Street Gallery, San Francisco, CA.

1974
Neighbors, Jackson Street Gallery, San Francisco, CA.
Gum San Haak, KRON-TV broadcast of Loni Ding's film featuring Asian American artists, San Francisco, CA.

Awards/Commissions:

2008
Creative Work Fund Grant - Kearny Street Workshop

2006
Mills College/California Council on Humanities commission

2005
National Endowment for the Arts award

1990
Festival 2000 Artist Commission Award

1982
California Arts Council Artist-in-Residence

Teaching/Art Related Experience:

2003-04
Photo contributor, *Hyphen* Magazine, San Francisco

1997
Photo Lecturer, Bob Hsiang Studios, San Francisco

1986
Guest Speaker, Photo Series, Chinese Culture Center, San Francisco

1982
Photo Instructor, California Arts Council Artist-in-Residenc, Kearny Street Workshop, San Francisco

1974-76
Photographer, CETA Program, M.H. de Young Museum, San Francisco

1973
Photo Instructor, Kearny Street Workshop, San Francisco

Selected Published Work:

2008
Hajratwala, Minal, "Leaving India," Houghton Mifflin Harcourt, Boston

2003
Moyers, Bill. "Becoming American," WNET-Channel 13, New York City
Hyphen Magazine - Summer, Fall, San Francisco
Nakanishi, Don and James Lai. "Asian American Politics," Roman and Littlefield

2002
Ling, Amy. "Yellow Light," Temple University Press, Philadelphia

2001
Louie, Steve. "The Movement and the Moment," UCLA Press, Los Angeles
Adler, Howard. "The Whole World is Watching," Berkeley Art Center Association, Berkeley
Wong, William. "Yellow Journalist," Temple University Press, Philadelphia

1997
Lee, Josephine. "Performing Asian America," Temple University Press, Philadelphia

1994
Saunders, Pat and Tajiri, Rea. "Passion for Justice," Video, New York City

1993
Wei, William. "The Asian American Movement," Temple University Press, Philadelphia

1992
"Pursuing the Wild Bamboo Provides Intimate Glimpse of 6 Artists," *Asian Week*, San Francisco
"Pursuing the Wild Bamboo: Portraits of Asian American Artists," Kearny Street Workshop, San Francisco

1982
Eisenberg, Barbara. "California Theater Annual," Performing Arts Network

DONNA KEIKO OZAWA

Donna Keiko Ozawa is a visual artist who makes kinetic and viewer-activated sculpture and installation with recycled materials, sound, electronics and whatever she can scavenge or figure out. Her work tends to ruminate—at times humorously—upon her personal anxieties about political and cultural dilemmas. Prior to receiving her MFA from the School of the Art Institute of Chicago, she worked as a community organizer and youth advocate. She is a co-founder of LYRIC, the Lavender Youth Recreation and Information Center, the nation's largest LGBTQQ youth organization. She is also a drummer and electric bassist gigging with local bands. She was born and raised in San Francisco, lives in Berkeley, keeps a well-equipped studio in Oakland, and stores stuff (like 180,000 used chopsticks) in Richmond.
www.donnaozawa.com

Selected Exhibitions:

(Solo shows)
2005
The Waribashi Project: San Francisco, Japantown Center, San Francisco, CA.
The Waribashi Project: San Francisco/ Project Launch & Works-in-progress, United Nations World Environment Day, Red Ink Studios, San Francisco, CA.

2001
Work from the Dump, Selected works by Donna Keiko Ozawa, Artist-in-Residence Program, Sanitary Fill Company, San Francisco, CA.

1999
Transformation/Possibility: The Waribashi Project, Design Festa, Tokyo, Japan.

(Two-person/Group shows)
2007
Things That Go Up and Down, Office Gallery, San Francisco, CA.

2005
Sociedad de Vida, A 15-Year Retrospective of the Norcal Artist Residency at the Dump, Steven Wolf Fine Arts, San Francisco, CA.
Pirated, Kearney Street Workshop, San Francisco, CA.

2004
Roadside Elixir, Headlands Center for the Arts, Open House, Sausalito, CA.

2003
The Art Health Fair, (curated and exhibited in) two shows, Oakland Museum of California, Oakland, CA.
Sliv & Dulet Present: The Summer Line, New Langton Center for the Arts, San Francisco, CA.

2003
Artworks: The Work of Art Handlers, Chela Gallery, Baltimore, MD.

2002
Cycles, Recycles, Creative Arts Center Gallery, City of Sunnyvale, Sunnyvale, CA.
Art That Moves, San Francisco Mechanical, Kinetic and Electronic Arts Festival, Crucible Steel Gallery at CELLspace, San Francisco, CA.
Picking Up the Pieces, Euphrat Museum of Art, DeAnza College, Cupertino, CA.

2001
The Fine Art of Recycling, Selected works by Sanitary Fill Company Artists in Residence, Transamerica Corporation, San Francisco, CA.
Selected works by Sanitary Fill Company Artists in Residence, One Market Plaza, San Francisco, CA.

1999
American American, Indigo Som/ Donna Keiko Ozawa, Crucible Steel Gallery at CELL, San Francisco, CA.

1997
Living with Television, Gallery 2, School of the Art Institute of Chicago, Chicago, IL.

Residencies:

2004
Bay Area Discovery Museum, Sausalito, CA.

2003
Oakland Museum of California, Fall Head Royce Lower School, Oakland, CA.

2001

Sanitary Fill Company, San Francisco, CA.

1999

Japan-U.S. Community Education and Exchange (JUCEE) Program, Design Festa, Tokyo, Japan

Selected Awards:

2007

San Francisco Foundation Matching Grant, San Francisco, CA.
Creative Work Fund, San Francisco, CA.

2005

LEF Foundation, San Francisco, CA.
Columbia Foundation Grant, San Francisco, CA.

Selected Reviews/Press:

2006

Leavenworth, Stuart. "Editorial Notebook: Chopsticks stick it to the world's forests," *Sacramento Bee*, March 26.

2005

Ansite, Katy. "Seeing Things/ The Waribashi Project," Kitchen *Sink* Magazine, September, Vol. 3, Issue 3.
"New Exhibit to Draw Attention to How Used Chopsticks Create Environmental Waste," *Nichi Bei Times*, San Francisco, August 25, Number 16, 189.

2005

Nakao, Annie. "Sculptor makes a point with more than a few pairs of chopsticks—60,000 of them to be precise," *San Francisco Chronicle/ SFGate.com*, June 4, Photos by Mark Constantini.
"'Waribashi Project' Raises Awareness of Environment," *Hokubei Mainichi*, May 17.
"Festival in San Francisco for UN Environment Day," Travel section, *New York Times*, May 1.
Buckner, Clark. "'Sociedad de Vida' at Steven Wolf Fine Arts," *Artweek,* Vol. 36, Issue 7, September.
Tunks, Jane, "Art Bandits, What's stealing and what's not, in 'Pirated: A Post Asian Perspective,'" *SF Weekly*, San Francisco, May 4.

2004

Taylor, Jiro. "The Waribashi Conundrum," *JapanVisitor.com*.
Davis, Kevin. "Don't worry, be happy: Artist Donna Ozawa at the Oakland Museum," *Bay Area Reporter*.

"'Art Health Fair' at Oakland Museum," *Hokubei Mainichi*.

2003

Boer, Joan. "The Artist Is In," *Art Guild News*, September/ October.

2002

Che, I-Chun. "Gallery displays recycled art," *The Cupertino Courier* and *The Sun*.

1999

"'American American' at Crucible Steel Gallery," Berin Golonu, *Artweek*, April, Vol. 30, Issue 4. *Asahi Newspaper*, Morning Edition, Tokyo, Japan, June 18, (featured photo).

Education:

1997

MFA, Sculpture/Studio Arts, School of the Art Institute of Chicago, Chicago, IL.

1986

BA, Latin American Studies and Spanish, Mount Holyoke College, South Hadley, MA.

CHRISTINE WONG YAP

Christine Wong Yap is a visual artist who makes sculptures, installations, works on paper and multiples to investigate optimism and pessimism. She has exhibited widely, locally, and recently in Japan, the Philippines and England. Her work is in the Alameda County Art Collection. Recently she received the Center for Cultural Innovation's Investing in Artists grant. Born in California, she holds a BFA and MFA from the California College of the Arts and has led several community mural projects around the country. She lives in Oakland, CA and works as an Affiliate Artist at the Headlands Center for the Arts. *www.christinewongyap.com*

Born:

1977 Santa Rosa, California

Selected Exhibitions:

2008

Sorry, Two-person exhibition. Frey Norris Gallery, San Francisco, CA
Dark Into Light, Solo project space exhibition. Swarm Gallery, Oakland, CA.

2007

FRED festival, Cumbria, UK.
Moving Cultures, Euphrat Museum, Cupertino, CA.
Galleon Trade, Green Papaya Art Projects, Quezon City, Philippines. Curated by Jenifer K. Wofford.
Centennial Graduate Exhibition, California College of the Arts, San Francisco, CA.
Beats Per Minute, Museum of Craft & Folk Art, San Francisco, CA. Curated by Julio C. Morales.
Supermarket 2007, Koh-i-noor booth, Copenhagen, Sweden.
Alumni at the Centennial, Oliver Art Center, Oakland, CA. Juried by Julie Joyce & Jo Lauria.

2006

Immediate Futures, San Francisco Arts Commission Gallery, San Francisco, CA.
Print Exchange, Osaka University of Arts, Osaka, Japan / Oliver Arts Center, Oakland, CA.
The Home Show, Kearny Street Workshop, San Francisco, CA.
Fling. SOMArts, San Francisco, CA.

2005

Justice Matters, Berkeley Art Center, Berkeley, CA.
CirCA Now, Oakland Museum Restaurant Gallery, Oakland, CA.

2004

Paper Bullets, Intersection for the Arts, San Francisco, CA.
APAture, Kearny Street Workshop / SOMArts, San Francisco, CA.

2003

To Conjure a Language, ProArts Gallery, Oakland, CA.
Visible Resistance. Asian Arts Initiative, Philadelphia, PA.

2002

Magician's Day Off, Euphrat Museum, Cupertino, CA.
War? What is it Good For? Asian Resource Gallery, Oakland, CA.

2001

A.I.R. Gallery. New York, NY.
Limited Edition, Kearny Street Workshop / Asia Pacific Cultural Center, Oakland, CA.

2000

Christine Wong, Asian Resource Gallery, Oakland, CA.

1999

Y2K, Southern Exposure, San Francisco, CA.

Public Collections:

Alameda County Art Collection, Alameda County, CA.

Awards:

2008

Investing in Artists grant, Center for Cultural Innovation, San Francisco, CA.

2007

Affiliate Artist, Headlands Center for the Arts, Sausalito, CA.

2006

Murphy Fellowship in the Fine Arts, San Francisco Foundation. Juried by Anuradha Vikram, Julio Morales and Jerome Reyes.

2005

Hamaguchi Endowed Scholarship, CCA, San Francisco, CA.

2002

Sister of Fire Award,Women of Color Resource Center, Oakland, CA.

2000

Local Hero, Best of the Bay Awards, *San Francisco Bay Guardian.*

1999

Grantee. Active Element Foundation, New York, NY.

Education:

2007

MFA. California College of the Arts (CCA), San Francisco, CA.

1998

BFA. CCA, San Francisco, CA.

Bibliography:

2008

Light, Claire. "Art Review: Christine Wong Yap: Activist Imagination." *KQED.org* website, Arts & Culture section, Visual Arts section. March 9.
Ritchie, Andy. "Gallery Hop Around Town with Andy Richie—Dark into Light." *Artslant* San Francisco, February 24.

2007

Dumancas, Pedro. "'Galleon Trade,' Fil-Am Exodus Back to the Motherland." *Philippine Daily Inquirer.* August 5.
Harmanci, Reyhan. "Galleon Trade: Ship Launch!" *San Francisco Chronicle.* June 28.
Killian, Kevin. "Studio Visit." *Mirage #4/Period(ical)*, Issue #138, February 2007.

Meeker, Cheryl. "CCA's 2007 Graduate Exhibition." *Stretcher.org.* May 11.
"Fred: An Art Invasion." *Arts Update.* Issue 59. Cumbria, UK: Sept./Oct./Nov. 2007

2006

Nguyen Qui Duc. "Asian Americans' Notions of Home." *Pacific Time*, KQED, July 13.

2003

Koppman, Debra. "Review: To Conjure a Language." *Artweek*, March.
Lin, Serena. "Artists Speak Out Against the War." *Tea Party* Magazine. Issue #13.
Yuen, Jennifer May. "Bay Area Artists Speak out for Peace in New Exhibit." *AsianWeek*, February 28.

2001

Inglis, Titiana Leung. "Young Artists show at the Asia Pacific." *Oakland Tribune*, March 31.
"*BLU Magazine.* Profile with several photos." The Radical Pacific Issue.

2000

Zoll, Daniel. "Local Hero: Christine Wong." *San Francisco Bay Guardian*, July 26.

SAMANTHA CHANSE

Samantha Chanse has been involved with Kearny Street Workshop since 2001, when she joined KSW's *APAture* festival planning committee as a volunteer. She served as the *APAture* coordinator in 2002, joining staff later that year to eventually serve as program and artistic director. During her years at KSW, she has curated dozens of programs and exhibitions, and has edited several KSW Press publications, in addition to her other staff responsibilities. She has been involved with a number of other Bay Area organizations, including Asian American Theater Company and Intersection for the Arts, and was a volunteer co-director of Locus Arts for five years. A native of New York City who moved to San Francisco in 2001, she is also a produced playwright and a writer/ performer.

Kearny Street Workshop (KSW) was founded in 1972 in San Francisco's Chinatown/Manilatown neighborhood. Much of its art and definition were derived from the struggles and issues surrounding that neighborhood: the struggle for low-income housing; the strikes of garment and electrical union workers; the connection with the tenants of the International Hotel, where KSW was housed until our eviction from the site in 1977. The early 1970s was a time of growth for the Asian American Movement; all across the country new groups were forming that addressed issues of health care, identity, history and cultural pride. Artistically, it was a fertile time of exploration. KSW was part of a grassroots art movement that pioneered innovative and influential forms of Asian American art, including Asian American jazz, small press publications, silkscreen posters and large-scale public murals.

Noting a scarcity of original art coming out of Chinatown, Jim Dong, Lora Foo, and Mike Chin founded KSW in August 1972 with funds from the National Endowment for the Arts, the San Francisco Neighborhood Arts Program, and the Chinatown-North Beach Youth Council. Located in the International Hotel at 854 Kearny Street, KSW was starting to offer different forms of creative expression to the Chinatown community. Workshops were offered in silk screening, sewing, modern dance, photography, ceramics, drawing, sewing, jewelry making, guitar, leather craft, needlepoint, and video. Even boxing and tai chi were offered. In 1974 KSW opened the Jackson Street Gallery, located on the Jackson Street side of the International Hotel. The space, formerly the Hungry i, was large enough to hold a huge gallery and performance space, as well as a meeting area. KSW then began to produce exhibitions and performances.

Once called the "model grassroots program" by the NEA, KSW quickly became a drop-in center for artists and community members. We also extended our work into the Chinatown community by conducting art sessions at schools and children's and senior centers. "In those first few summers, a few hundred kids would go through the workshop in one week. At the peak, we had five to seven classes every day," said founder Jim Dong.

KSW was the first to do a mural in Chinatown. KSW artists painted a mural in Commodore Stockton Elementary School after a teacher observed that a lot of the teachers did not know that much about Chinese American history. KSW artists also executed the long mural on the Jackson Street side of the International Hotel. During the period following the fall of the I-Hotel, KSW moved to a small storefront in North Beach. After a short stay, KSW moved back to Chinatown — to another hotel, next door to a senior meals program. There, daily interaction with the senior citizens who came to eat their lunch provided the inspiration for KSW's artists, writers, and photographers. KSW's small press published books of poetry and photography, and we started presenting more outside of the facility. A short while later, priced out of Chinatown, KSW settled into small units inside the California Flower Market.

In 1981, KSW started the Asian American Jazz Festival, which was held at various venues in San Francisco before it formed a partnership with the Asian Art Museum. Under the directorship of KSW director Mark Izu, the Asian American Jazz Festival flourished. The event became a vehicle for talented artists to showcase and promote their works. Many noted Asian American musicians, writers, and visual artists could trace their career paths back to KSW. KSW produced the Asian American Jazz Festival for 17 years before turning it over to another group.

KSW: A BRIEF HISTORY

In March 1995, KSW received its 501(c)(3) status, shortly after Nancy Hom was appointed executive director. Nancy strengthened KSW's infrastructure, formalized a board of directors, redirected the organization's programming, and expanded its resources. She formed relationships with other community groups within and beyond the Asian American community. At this time, KSW moved from its cramped quarters in the California Flower Market to South Park, soon to be a mecca for new media mavens. At this point Claire Light joined KSW staff as program and office manager, and along with Hom, had a tremendous impact on KSW's programs for the next half decade.

By the mid-1990s KSW's founding core had become less involved in the organization and a new generation of artists was coming of age. KSW formed KSW-Next in July 1998 to offer the APA community's next generation of adults their own space to grow as artists and activists. Originally comprised of artists aged 18 to 35, but now open to and involving emerging artists and arts organizers of all ages, KSW-Next is a training ground and network for our community's emerging artists. Guided by KSW's mission, its members curate and organize our annual festival, *APAture: A Window on the Art of Asian Pacific Americans*, in its 10th year in 2008, and one of the nation's largest gatherings of APA artists.

The dot-com boom forced KSW to move again in 2000, this time to SomArts Cultural Center, where our offices were housed for the next five years. At SomArts, we presented readings, exhibitions, screenings, workshops, and other programs, including six of our *APAture* festivals.

In the summer of 2005, KSW moved again to our current home, KSW's space180, on the third floor of 180 Capp Street in the Mission District. The space was secured along with space180 partner groups Locus Arts, another multidisciplinary Asian Pacific American arts organization, and APA-design group Tactile Pictures. Since moving to space180, KSW has provided a home for thousands of artists and arts supporters. Today at space180 and around San Francisco, with artistic director Samantha Chanse and executive director Ellen Oh, KSW continues to engage and enrich our communities, offering: ongoing workshops; literary readings, musical performances, exhibitions, and other arts presentations; our annual *APAture* festival; publications through our small press; and collaborations with other groups.

From its beginnings in the International Hotel, KSW has grown to a vital organization with a focus on intergenerational, cross-cultural activities that honor our historical and cultural heritage. We also support the efforts of artists who desire to find grounding through community involvement, and nurture a new generation of artists on the cutting edge of artistic expression. No longer in a singular Asian American neighborhood, KSW serves a wide range of constituents. Our work continues to provide a crucial venue for untold stories and access for APA artists in our community. All of our programs share a common purpose to explore and provide insight to contemporary Asian Pacific American issues through art.

KSW's mission is to produce and present art that enriches and empowers APA communities. Our vision is to achieve a more just society by connecting APA artists with community members to give voice to our cultural, historical, and contemporary issues.

www.kearnystreet.org

KSW STAFF AND BOARD
Ellen Oh, *Executive Director*
Samantha Chanse, *Artistic Director*

BOARD OF DIRECTORS
Vid Prabhakaran, *President*
Amy Lam, *Vice President*
Felicia Sze, *Secretary*
Lyman Yip, *Treasurer*

Chris Bucoy Brown	Amy Lam
Samantha Chanse	Myron Lee
Gerry Chow	Nirmala Nataraj
Yasmine Gomez	Ellen Oh

The *Activist Imagination* project is made possible in part by a grant from the Creative Work Fund through support from the Walter and Elise Haas Fund, The William and Flora Hewlett Foundation, and the James Irvine Foundation. *Activist Imagination* is also supported in part by a grant from the San Francisco Foundation and by KSW's members and individual donors.

CREATIVEWORKFUND

THE SAN FRANCISCO FOUNDATION
The Community Foundation of the Bay Area

Kearny Street Workshop (KSW) is the oldest multidisciplinary Asian Pacific American arts organization in the country. Founded in 1972, KSW's mission is to produce and present art that enriches and empowers Asian Pacific American communities. Our vision is to achieve a more just society by connecting APA artists with community members to give voice to our historical, cultural, and contemporary issues. KSW offers a range of programming, including public presentations and exhibitions, publications, workshops, and an annual arts festival. For more information visit www.kearnystreet.org.

Christine Wong Yap gives special thanks to California Ethnic and Multicultural Archives (CEMA) and Director Sal Guerena; Zand Gee, Nancy Hom, Leland Wong and all the early KSW artists; Sam Chanse, Jon Sueda, Sophine Lim; Norman Bock; Elizabeth Travelslight; Michael Yap

Donna Keiko Ozawa gives special thanks to Indigo Som, Nancy Hom, and Calvin Roberts.

Bob Hsiang gives special thanks to Samantha Chanse, Connie Hwong, Christine Wong Yap, Donna Keiko Ozawa, Nancy Hom, Ben Pease, Lenore Chin, all the AI subjects included in the project, The New Lab, and all the volunteers who helped realize the exhibit.

Kearny Street Workshop and Samantha Chanse give special thanks to Bob Hsiang, Donna Keiko Ozawa, Christine Wong Yap, Nancy Hom, Norman Bock, Jon Sueda, Sophine Lim, Jenifer Wofford, the Creative Work Fund, The San Francisco Foundation, Nancy Hom, Oscar Peñaranda, Min Paek, Alison Lee Satake, Eric Mar, Favianna Rodriguez, Robynn Takayama, Le Tim Ly, Diana Pei Wu, Wei Ming Dariotis, Pireeni Sundaralingam, Erika Shuch, Ron Muriera, Carlos Villa, Kevin B. Chen, Bob Hanamura, Claire Light, Vid Prabhakaran, Gerry Chow, Connie Hwong, Ellen Oh, Amy Lam, Catherine Chanse, Laura Valdez, Nicholas Ng, Yen Nguyen, Carolyn Yang, Jay Jao, Derek Chung, Mark Baugh-Sasaki, Josh McDermott, Ari Solomon, Rissa Duque and the Manilatown Center, Valencia Printing, the KSW Board, and KSW's donors, members, and volunteers.

Editor: Samantha Chanse
Copy Editors: Ellen Oh, Connie Hwong
Contributors: Samantha Chanse, Kevin B. Chen, Bob Hsiang, Donna Keiko Ozawa, Christine Wong Yap
Designed by Sophine Lim and Jon Sueda
Printed in Canada by Westcan Printing Group

Photo Credits:
Pages 2-3: Kearny Street Workshop artists, including Zand Gee, Nancy Hom, Jack Loo, Mitsui Murai, Leland Wong and others. *An exhibition of reproductions of Kearny Street Workshop Posters, curated by Christine Wong Yap* (installation view). 1974–1983, digital prints, 10 x 10 x 10 feet. Photo by Christine Wong Yap.
Pages 4-5: Donna Keiko Ozawa's *Robbie was there II, Robbie was there I;* Christine Wong Yap's *untitled* site-specific window intervention; Donna Keiko Ozawa's *Weather Buddha* and *Sheep House I.* Photo by Bob Hsiang.
Pages 6-7: Bob Hsiang's *Portrait of 13 Activists.* Photo by Bob Hsiang.
Page 8: Christine Wong Yap's *Untitled* (installation view) 2008, site-specific window intervention: window tint, gels, tape, 9 x 7 feet. Photo by Bob Hsiang.
Pages 42-43 left to right: Carlos Villa, Ron Muriera, Pireeni Sundaralingam, and Erika Shuch, at 3/27/2008 discussion. Photo by Derek Chung.
Page 44: Bob Hsiang at the 4/24/2008 artist talk. Photo by Derek Chung.
Pages 45: Donna Keiko Ozawa at the 4/24/2008 artist talk. Photo by Derek Chung.
Pages 46: Christine Wong Yap at the 4/24/2008 artist talk. Photo by Derek Chung.

Kearny Street Workshop Press | San Francisco
©Copyright 2008

To learn more, request reprint rights, or order copies of this or other KSW publications, please contact KSW:

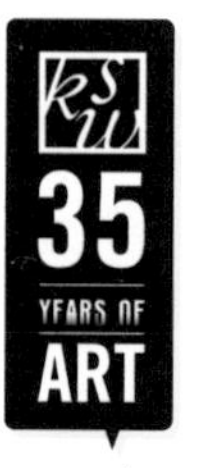

KEARNY STREET WORKSHOP
180 Capp Street, #5
San Francisco, CA 94110
415.503.0520 | 415.503.0547
www.kearnystreet.org

ISBN 978-0-9797707-2-2
Library of Congress Control Number: 2008926694